Getting Started in AA

Getting Started in AA*

Hamilton B.

*This work contains only the ideas, experiences, and suggestions collected by the author. It is not an official publication of Alcoholics Anonymous World Services, Inc., nor does it necessarily represent the policies or practices of the AA Fellowship.

HAZELDEN®

Hazelden
Center City, Minnesota 55012-0176

LIBRARY OF CONGRESS CATALOGING-IN-PUBLICATION DATA
B., Hamilton.
   Getting started in AA / by Hamilton B.
      p.   cm.
   Includes bibliographical references and index.
   ISBN 1-56838-091-7
   1. Alcoholics Anonymous—Handbooks, manuals, etc. 2. Alcoholics—
Rehabilitation—Handbooks, manuals, etc.   I. Title.
HV5278.B3 1995
362.29'286—dc20   95-24001
                                                                              CIP

EDITOR'S NOTE
   Hazelden offers a variety of information on chemical dependency and related areas. Our publications do not necessarily represent Hazelden's programs, nor do they officially speak for any Twelve Step organization.
   The Twelve Steps and Twelve Traditions are reprinted with permission of Alcoholics Anonymous World Services, Inc. Permission to reprint this material does not mean that Alcoholics Anonymous has reviewed or approved the contents of this publication, nor that AA agrees with the views expressed herein. The views expressed herein are solely those of the author. AA is a program of recovery from alcoholism. Use of the Twelve Steps in connection with programs and activities that are patterned after AA, but that address other problems, does not imply otherwise.

   The following publishers have generously given permission to use quotations from copyrighted works: From *Getting Better: Inside Alcoholics Anonymous,* copyright 1988, by William Morrow & Company, Inc. Reprinted by permission of the author. From *Bill W.,* copyright 1975, by Robert Thomsen. Reprinted by permission of HarperCollins Publishers, Inc. From *Lois Remembers,* copyright 1979, by Al-Anon Family Group Headquarters, Inc. Reprinted by permission of Al-Anon Family Group Headquarters, Inc.

To Miss Helen Greenwood (1907–1995) with profound gratitude. A gifted high school teacher who taught writing and a love of English with devotion, dedication, and inspiration, she forever changed my view of the world and of myself. *Deo non fortuna.*

Contents

Preface

When I was new to Alcoholics Anonymous in August 1978, I was told: "Don't drink, go to meetings, work the Steps, and find a sponsor." Then I was given a copy of the Big Book, *Alcoholics Anonymous*, and told to read it. I couldn't read the first part because I was too jittery to concentrate. I did read the stories in the back during the late night hours when I couldn't sleep. Much later, I was given a copy of the AA publication *Living Sober* and told to read it, too, because it contained some practical suggestions for staying sober.

When I first came to AA, I was told: "Don't drink, go to meetings, read the Big Book, work the Steps, and find a sponsor."

The longer I have been sober, the more I have come to value the practical insights that AA members lovingly passed on to me in those early days. Somehow, I couldn't seem to find that wisdom in the Big Book, although, of course, it was there. Instead, I needed the more immediate, distilled version that came from the lips of other AA members in countless discussions and one-on-one conversations.

When I began to sponsor newcomers myself, I realized that I didn't have the time or memory to pass on to them all the suggestions I had been given. AA's collective "experience, strength, and hope" contains many practical ideas that can help us from the beginning. But no single book provided a summary of that wisdom in a condensed, easily understood form. The Big Book often proved as difficult for my spon-sees as it had for me in the early days of sobriety. Where could they turn? After a decade and a half of recovery, I gave some thought to preparing a small book to help them.

The result is *Getting Started in AA.* What began as a few notes for my sponsees has (in the best alcoholic tradition) grown into some-thing larger and more complex. Even so, I have still tried to keep the book simple and faithful to its original concept. It is a book for those starting out in AA and for their sponsors. It is also a book for AA members who want to know more about their Fellowship.

The suggestions in *Getting Started in AA* are not original with me. Everything in the book came from AA members, meetings, and publications. But everything is filtered through my perception. This book is about AA, but it does not speak for AA. The only real author-ities in AA are the Big Book, *The Twelve Steps and Twelve Traditions,* other Conference-approved literature, and decisions of the AA General Service Conference. The General Service Conference speaks for all of AA as our elected voice. This book is not Conference-approved. It is, in the final analysis, merely my opinion. I may well have gotten some of it wrong. In the best AA tradition, use what you can and leave the rest.

**In the best AA tradition,
use what you can.**

There is no way that I can adequately thank Alcoholics Anonymous for having given me my life. All that I can do is try to be there for other alcoholics, as recovering alcoholics were there for me in my first scary, wonderful, terrifying, exhilarating days in AA. This book is part of being there for other alcoholics. I hope it helps you.

I especially want to thank my sponsor, David S., for his experi-ence, strength, and hope over the years and for introducing me to the delightful phrase "grand sponsor" to refer to our sponsor's sponsor. He was kind enough to read this manuscript and to make some significant suggestions. I also want to thank my spiritual advisor, Father Tom, who is not an alcoholic but who understands the disease and who has contributed immeasurably to my spiritual growth. I love both these men, and I will always be grateful to them.

Alcoholics Anonymous is a "we" program. I get drunk; *we* stay sober.

I also want to thank the following members of the Fellowship who have played such an integral part in my sobriety (in alphabetical order): Anne L. B., Allan C., Mark G., Tim G., the late Tom G. (who gave me my first Big Book), Ann H., Harry L., the late Sandy S., and Marijane V. Also, in another part of the country, Ed C., Abigail G., Lauder G., Hal M., Ed S., and Steve W.

I want to thank all my sponsees (past and present) from whom I have learned more than I have taught, but especially Andy B., Brian B., Byron B., Chris D., John K., David L., Henry S., Dave T., and Warren T.

Finally, I want to thank some special people in my life who are connected in one way or another with Twelve Step recovery and who will know who they are: Carol B., Herb B., Lane C., Kathy G., Pat M., Judith N., and Patti P.

I am very grateful to my editor at Hazelden for his keen interest in this book and for his suggestions that have added immeasurably to its usefulness. I am also grateful to Cathy Broberg, my manuscript editor, for the many changes she suggested that significantly improved the manuscript. I also want to thank Alcoholics Anonymous World Services, Inc. for it generous permission to quote so extensively from AA sources.

The path we take is ours to trod but not completely ours to design. The Road of Happy Destiny has many twists and turns as well as broad highways and an occasional cul-de-sac. But it's still the best road in town. I hope to see you on it. God bless and keep you.

The Easy Way to Use This Book

Getting Started in AA is not a book that has to be read from the front to the back.

Start reading wherever you want.

The book is divided into several parts so that you can skip to the subjects that interest you most. Later, if you want, you can come back to the rest. The table of contents lists the topics covered in the book. There you can find the subject you want to read about first and get started right away.

**Check the table of contents for a
list of topics covered in the book.**

Parts 1 through 3 of the book are about AA basics, AA meetings and groups, and anonymity. Chapter 17, "Finding the Right Meeting for You," and chapters 18–20 are important for newcomers who are gay or lesbian, people of color, dually diagnosed with an emotional disorder, dually addicted to drugs other than alcohol, or recently released from prison. It discusses some AA traditions and special interest meetings that will help you get a good start.

Part 4 is called "The Survival Guide." It has three chapters that offer practical suggestions for staying sober. Chapter 23 answers a bunch of questions that newcomers often have. Chapter 24 gives you seventy-five ways to stay sober. And chapter 25 is about how to have a good time without alcohol.

Part 5 has four appendices and is a kind of reference section. It contains a short history of AA, a section on the writing of the Big Book, a group of passages from AA literature that are often quoted in meetings (if you want to read the AA Promises, for example, you will find them here), and a listing of other books about AA.

There is also a glossary of common terms you'll run into at AA meetings and an index at the end of the book with the page numbers of key subjects so that you can find a given topic quickly.

**Check the index in the back
for page numbers of specific
topics arranged alphabetically.**

The single purpose of this book is to teach you about AA and, through that teaching, to help you stay sober. Use the book in whatever way is most effective for you.

PART 1

AA BASICS

Alcoholics Anonymous (AA) is a simple program for complex people. Because something is simple doesn't mean that it's easy—only that it's not complicated. AA's program of recovery is based on twelve simple Steps. In addition to the Steps, every newcomer (or old-timer) who wants to stay sober is given these traditional suggestions:

1. *Don't drink.*
2. *Go to meetings.*
3. *Read the Big Book.*
4. *Work the Steps*
5. *Call your sponsor.*
6. *Say your prayers.*
7. *Help another alcoholic.*

These seven actions are supported by many AA living strategies that are expressed in simple slogans. Here are some of the most important slogans:

1. *Put sobriety first.*
2. *Take sobriety and life one day at a time.*
3. *Keep it simple.*
4. *Remember that it's the first drink that gets us drunk.*
5. *Think the drink through.*
6. *Avoid slippery places.*

No description of AA basics would be complete without the Serenity Prayer. It is one of the most powerful tools available to us. Many people— even those outside of AA—believe it contains the secret to a happy and successful life. Understanding and using the Serenity Prayer has saved many alcoholics from relapse and has made their lives more peaceful and joyous.

THE SERENITY PRAYER

God, grant me the serenity
to accept the things I cannot change,
the courage to change the things I can,
and the wisdom to know the difference.

When we're new to AA, we have a lot to learn. Some of the things we hear in AA meetings may seem contradictory. And some of them are. What is said in meetings about AA is merely an AA member's opinion. It may be right, and it may be wrong. Only AA can speak for itself. AA speaks through its textbook, Alcoholics Anonymous *(the Big Book)*, Twelve Steps and Twelve Traditions *(the Twelve and Twelve)*, and other Conference-approved literature. By reading these books yourself, you won't be misled by somebody else's misunderstanding of AA principles.

Within reason, we are entitled to "take what we want and leave the rest" as we listen in AA meetings. Even the Steps, of course, are only "suggested," but they are suggested for those who want to get and stay sober. People who don't need to get sober don't need to work the Steps. In the end, we make our own decisions about what is useful for us, but we must be careful. Our judgment is generally poor when we come into AA. We don't want to hear some of the things we need to hear. When I came into the Fellowship, there was a saying for newcomers that was more common than now. It was a slogan that was often repeated for my benefit. The expression was "Take the cotton out of your ears and put it in your mouth." It meant that I should listen rather than talk so much or raise so many objections. Contrary to what I thought at the time, I had a lot to learn. One way to learn was to listen. That piece of advice is still sound for newcomers.

**Take the cotton out of your ears
and put it in your mouth.**

Yet, it isn't quite enough just to listen. We are asked to listen with an open mind. Instead of "knowing it all" and insisting on doing things our own way, we are asked to be open to something new. It is also suggested that we pray for willingness—willingness to listen, to learn, to change. We'll have to do all that to stay sober.

**HOW IT WORKS:
H: Honesty
O: Open-mindedness
W: Willingness**

Chapter 1

Don't Drink

Recovery from alcoholism requires complete abstinence from alcohol. "Abstinence" means "not having any." Alcoholics Anonymous, therefore, is about *not drinking*. Abstinence applies to all mood-altering chemicals. So whenever you read "don't drink," you can add "or use." There is no other way to recover from the disease of alcoholism. As alcoholics, whenever we drink, we activate our disease and ultimately lose control over how much we drink. We may drink too much today or tomorrow or next week. But we will do it again. "Alcoholism" means having "impaired control over alcohol." That's what alcoholism is. Those are the cold, hard facts.

**Alcoholics have lost the
ability to control how much
alcohol they drink.**

AA gives us the power to choose to recover from our alcoholism, but we still have to make that choice. The Big Book, the Twelve Steps, the meetings, our sponsor, our relationship with our Higher Power, and all the other elements of the AA recovery program are designed to help us stay sober. Alcoholics Anonymous is a powerful resource to use against our disease—and it works.

No matter what, don't drink. The old saying is "even if your ass falls off." Ultimately, everything comes down to that one choice. AA's entire program is geared to that one moment in which we make the decision to drink or not to drink.

**No matter what,
don't drink.**

For some of us, the compulsion to drink—and even the desire—was taken away immediately upon entering AA. For others, it was a matter of days, weeks, months, or even years. Why the timing is different among us is unknown. But even those who still wanted to drink after coming into AA were able to stay sober by working the AA program.

**There is no problem in life
that a drink will make better.**

**There is no problem in life
that a drink will not make worse.**

Based on our own experience and on the experience of others, we came to see that not one of our problems was solved by taking a drink. Sometimes a drink made us feel better temporarily, but the cost was high. And it never helped in the long run. On the other hand, none of us had really wanted "a" drink either. What we had wanted were many drinks that would make us high and help us forget our problems. And once we started, we often couldn't stop. We found that "one drink was too many and a thousand drinks were not enough." The only solution for us as alcoholics was not to take the first drink. AA enabled us to do just that.

**For an alcoholic, one drink
is too many and a thousand
drinks are not enough.**

Chapter 2

Go to Meetings

It is in Alcoholics Anonymous meetings throughout America that over one million AA members share their experience, strength, and hope with each another and find recovery.[1] AA meetings are very important to sobriety, especially early on. They are what much of this book is about.

There are more than one million AA members in America and more than two million worldwide.

When I came into AA years ago, it was suggested that I attend thirty meetings during my first thirty days of sobriety. At the time that suggestion seemed like an impossible task. When I objected to attending so many meetings, it was explained to me that I didn't have to do them all at once. The goal was to go to one meeting a day, thereby taking the idea of "thirty in thirty" one day at a time. Since I was afraid of drinking again, I did what I was told. I made one meeting a day and tried not to think about all the meetings I still had to make.

Today, the thirty-meeting goal has been expanded to ninety meetings during the first ninety days. "Ninety in ninety" gives us a running start in the AA program that makes a return to drinking less likely.

"Ninety in ninety" means to attend ninety meetings in the first ninety days of sobriety.

For us as newcomers, this concentration of AA meetings does the following:

1. Provides a cram course in the principles and ideas of AA's recovery program.
2. Provides emotional support for our recovery.
3. Reduces our loneliness and sense of isolation as we bond with fellow AA members in the meetings.
4. Gives us something to do at night (or during the day) when we used to be drinking, so that we are less likely to return to our old hangouts or old habits.
5. Gives us a new set of friends who will encourage us in sobriety, answer our questions, and help us stay in recovery.
6. Brings an orderliness to our lives to combat the chaos and fear that are often present in early sobriety.
7. Means a commitment to being teachable and to being willing to change.

In early sobriety, it pays to attend various AA meetings because every meeting is different. Each of us identifies more with some meetings than with others and with some people more than with others. For those of us who are gay or lesbian, African American or Spanish-speaking, dually diagnosed or dually addicted, or just getting out of prison, finding the right meeting can be especially important. If you didn't like the first AA meeting you attended, try another one and another one. Don't give up. Until we have visited many meetings, it is hard to appreciate how diverse AA really is. There's always a meeting somewhere that's right for us.

Whatever your background or special needs, there's probably an AA meeting for you.

Over time, most AA members find a "home group" to regularly attend and call "home." The members of our home group are like members of an extended family who have come to know us well in our sobriety. Most of us choose a home group because it has the meetings we like the best and feel the most comfortable attending. Regular attendance is important. In our home group, we find "a solid, continuing support system, friends, and, very often, a sponsor."[2] It is also where we "learn firsthand, through the group's workings, how to place 'principles before personalities' in the interest of carrying the A.A. message."[3] It is in our home group that we express our opinions through group conscience meetings and answer the call to service. It is our strongest link with the Fellowship.

> **Try many different meetings, but
> make one group your "Home Group"
> and attend it regularly.**

As a general rule, the longer our period of sobriety, the easier it is to determine how many meetings we need to attend each week. We work with our sponsor to decide how many meetings are necessary to maintain our serenity and protect our recovery. The number varies depending upon what is going on in our lives. During stressful periods, we increase the number of weekly meetings in order to maintain our desired comfort level. In peaceful times, we may slack off, but not below our minimum except in unusual circumstances.

> **There is no magic number
> of meetings to attend after
> the first ninety days.**

The AA Conference-approved book *Living Sober* says,

> We need to be as diligent in attending A.A. meetings as we were in drinking. What serious drinker ever let distance, or weather, or illness, or business, or guests, or being broke, or the hour, or anything else keep him or her from that really wanted drink? We cannot let anything keep us from A.A. meetings, either, if we really want to recover.

We have also found that going to meetings is not something to be done only when we feel the temptation to drink. We often get more good from the meetings by attending them when we feel fine and haven't so much as thought of drinking.[4]

**During stressful periods,
most of us increase our
attendance at meetings.**

At first, we attend meetings for what we can get out of them. In later sobriety, we discover another reason for going: to give back some of what we have been given. As our gratitude increases, we develop a greater sense of service to others. One of the ways we serve is by attending meetings.

Most of us feel that we never put into the meetings as much as we get out of them. How each of us continually draws more out of the Fellowship than we put into it is one of its great mysteries. The process suggests that a limitless supply of love and compassion is available to us. To me, it is one of the signs of a Higher Power.

**Attend AA meetings
regularly.**

Chapter 3

Read the Big Book

Alcoholics Anonymous, AA's basic textbook, is affectionately referred to as the "Big Book." It describes how the first one hundred people in AA stayed sober by working the Twelve Steps. The Big Book and the *Twelve Steps and Twelve Traditions* (the Twelve and Twelve) are the two primary resources of the AA recovery program.

The Big Book is the basic text of Alcoholics Anonymous.

The Big Book is divided into two unequal parts. The first quarter of the book describes AA's Twelve Step program. This part of the book was written by Bill Wilson, AA's cofounder. The last three-quarters of the book consists of forty-three personal stories written by recovered alcoholics. There are also six appendices.

Alcoholics Anonymous is a book of many levels—it can be read simply or at great depth. The longer we are sober, the more meaning it has for us, the deeper its insights, and the more powerful its wisdom. The answers to staying sober are contained within its pages. One of the first "assignments" most of us get as a new sponsee is to read the Big Book. A regular habit of *studying* the Big Book is very rewarding, and Big Book meetings can be helpful as well. For the newcomer, the Big Book is an introduction to the Twelve Step program. For the old-timer, it is a reminder of "how it works" and a way to strengthen sobriety.

**"How do I stay sober?"
is answered in the pages
of the Big Book.**

The Big Book was first published in 1939, so its language may seem dated at first. For example, the word "man" is used to refer to both men and women, and the pronouns "he" and "him" are used for the same purpose. But the Big Book is a historical document as well as a living guide to sobriety. Although some stories have been added or deleted over three editions, the first quarter of the present edition is almost identical to the first edition.

Everything that is said in meetings about what the AA program means, what AA stands for, and how the Twelve Steps work are purely the opinions of the speakers. But the Big Book is the opinion of AA itself. Its pages tell the story of how AA works and what we have to do to stay sober. The Big Book describes the path to sobriety and shows us how to walk it.

**Study the Big Book;
read it regularly.**

Chapter 4

Work the Steps

The Twelve Steps are introduced in chapter 5 of the Big Book with these words, "Rarely have we seen a person fail who has thoroughly followed our path."[1] "Our path" is the Twelve Steps. They are the heart of AA recovery. To work the AA program is to work the Twelve Steps. To live the AA program is to live the Twelve Steps. The sobriety of millions of alcoholics—and people with other addictions—is based on these twelve simple Steps. Programs like NA (Narcotics Anonymous), CA (Cocaine Anonymous), and OA (Overeaters Anonymous) have changed the wording slightly but still use the same basic Twelve Steps of recovery.

**The purpose of having meetings and
sponsors is to help us work the Twelve Steps.**

According to AA's cofounder Bill Wilson, the Twelve Steps "are a group of principles, spiritual in their nature, which, if practiced as a way of life, can expel the obsession to drink and enable the sufferer to become happily and usefully whole."[2] In other words, the Twelve Steps can keep us sober and happy. Dr. Bob, AA's cofounder, said, "Our Twelve Steps, when simmered down . . . resolve themselves into the words 'love' and 'service.'"[3]

The phrase "working a Step" or "taking a Step" is used in AA to describe the effort to understand and apply the principles of the Twelve Steps to our daily lives. It is not coincidental that the term "work" was chosen. It does take work to work the Steps. Bill Wilson writes, "All of the Twelve Steps require sustained and personal exertion to conform to their principles. . . ."[4] While recovery itself may be a gift, or by grace, the joy of recovery is earned by hard work focused on the Steps.

The Twelve Steps are traditionally worked under the guidance of a sponsor who has also worked them. In fact, it has been said that our sponsor's primary function is to help us work the Steps. The first phase of working a Step involves learning what the Step means. This phase is undertaken in a formal way with our sponsor. It includes reading the Big Book and the Twelve and Twelve, going to Twelve Step meetings, talking with other AA members, and studying the Step.

The first phase of working a Step is to understand what the Step means.

The second phase of working a Step involves changing our behavior in accordance with the principles of that Step. This phase could be called "applying the Step." It, too, requires the help of our sponsor. It also includes prayer and meditation, and daily, disciplined effort. To change the ingrained habits, thought patterns, and perceptions of a lifetime is not easy. Yet that is exactly what the second phase of working a Step is about.

The second phase of working a Step is to apply its principles to our daily lives.

Bill Wilson writes, "Alcoholics Anonymous does not demand that you believe anything. All of its Twelve Steps are but suggestions."[5] The suggested nature of AA's program of recovery allows us as alcoholics to make our own decision about working the Steps. Responsibility for working the program rests squarely on our own shoulders. No one will force us to do anything. The lack of rules, regulations, and requirements prevents us from rebelling against imagined authority.

**By calling the Twelve Steps "suggestions,"
AA left the decision to work them
entirely up to us.**

Although the Twelve Steps are suggestions, they do make up AA's recovery program. And it is AA's *only* program. Working them is, therefore, crucial to achieving and maintaining sobriety. Perhaps the best way to summarize the suggested nature of the Twelve Steps is this: You don't have to work the Twelve Steps unless you want to stay sober.

**You don't have to work the Twelve Steps
unless you want to stay sober.**

There is no prescribed timetable in the Big Book for taking the Steps. AA history tells us that Bill, Dr. Bob, and the early AA pioneers moved new AA members rapidly through the Steps. It makes sense to take the Steps as quickly as our circumstances will permit, as they are the key to sobriety. In the thirty-day residential treatment programs that multiplied in the 1980s, it was customary for the recovering alcoholic to have completed Step Five by the time he or she had finished treatment. The first Five Steps were thus taken in the first thirty days of sobriety.

**Because the Steps are the key to a
lasting and rewarding sobriety,
they should be worked as soon as possible.**

Even in today's more common outpatient programs, people are usually introduced to the first three Steps during treatment. The driving force of AA practice and tradition, therefore, seems to be in the direction of taking the Steps as rapidly as possible while still being thorough. Naturally, the timing will vary from person to person. However, someone who is new to AA should begin Step One immediately.

Graduates of both inpatient and outpatient programs need to continue working the Steps. It takes all twelve Steps to find real sobriety.
"Half measures availed us nothing."[6]

THE FIRST THREE STEPS

> *Step One: We admitted we were powerless over alcohol—that our
> lives had become unmanageable.*
>
> *Step Two: Came to believe that a Power greater than ourselves
> could restore us to sanity.*
>
> *Step Three: Made a decision to turn our will and our lives over to
> the care of God as we understood Him.*

It is said that AA's first three Steps can be summarized as "we
came," "we came to," "we came to believe." Through Step One, we
admitted our powerlessness over alcohol and *came* to AA. Through
Step Two, *we came to.* We came out of our denial, our fantasies, and
our emptiness to begin a spiritual awakening. Through Step Three, *we
came to believe* in a Power greater than ourselves to whose care we
turned over our lives.

The first three Steps have also been summarized as "I can't," "God
can," "I think I'll let Him." In the First Step, we admitted that we
could not recover from alcoholism by ourselves. In the Second Step,
we came to believe that God could keep us sober and restore us to sanity. In the Third Step, we turned our will and our lives over to God's
care for that purpose, letting Him do for us what we could not do by
ourselves.

**The first three Steps
can be summarized as
"I can't."
"God can."
"I think I'll let Him."**

Step One

With Step One, we admit to ourselves the exact nature of our problem. We are alcoholics. Alcoholics are people who are powerless over alcohol. As a result of that powerlessness, our lives had become unmanageable. The First Step is simple, but it is not necessarily easy to work yet. It is the only Step that the Big Book says we can work to perfection. All the other Steps are goals we aim for.

The First Step is so important because it describes our problem. If we can't see our problem, we can't find a solution to it. Our problem is powerlessness over alcohol and the resulting unmanageability of our lives. Some alcoholics think their problem is not their drinking, but their job or their spouse or their children or bad luck. If we think the problem is outside ourselves, we will look in the wrong place for its solution.

**The First Step is the only
one we can take perfectly.**

Step Two

In the Second Step, we discover that our situation is not hopeless and that our hope lies in recognizing a Power greater than ourselves. "Lack of power, that was our dilemma," says the Big Book. "We had to find a power by which we could live, and it had to be a *Power greater than ourselves.*" [7]

**In the Second Step, we discover
that our situation is not hopeless.**

The Second Step introduces another idea: our alcoholic behavior has been more than just unmanageable. It has been insane. One definition of "insanity" often heard in AA is this one: insanity is doing the same thing over and over and expecting different results.

**As drinking alcoholics, our lives
were more than unmanageable.
They were insane.**

Our Higher Power, working with us and through us, can restore us to sanity. Before we can be made willing to do our part, however, we have to ally ourselves with that Power greater than ourselves. This process is under way in the Second Step.

Step Three

The First Step led us to accept the fundamental problem we face as alcoholics: our powerlessness over alcohol and the unmanageability of our lives. The Second Step offered a solution: a Power greater than ourselves who could restore us to sanity. The Third Step tells us how to take advantage of that solution: by turning our will and our lives over to the care of that Power.

Bill Wilson wrote that "the effectiveness of the whole A.A. program will rest upon how well and earnestly we have tried to come to 'a decision to turn our will and our lives over to the care of God *as we understood Him.*'"[8]

God as we understand God is exactly that: the God of *our understanding,* even if it is no God at all. Whatever concept we ultimately choose is up to us as members of AA. But everyone has some concept of God or of no-God which affects his or her life. This Step merely asks us to examine that concept and describe it.

**All we need to know about
God is that we are not God.**

Step Three cannot be taken perfectly. Our experience has been that about as often as we "turn it over," we "take it back." We are continually making and remaking our decision. But we keep trying. This Step focuses our attention on the great tug-of-war we have with our Higher Power. Will it be the will of a Greater Power or ours that we follow in all our affairs?

Step Three asks us
to make a decision.

STEPS FOUR THROUGH TEN

Step Four: Made a searching and fearless moral inventory of ourselves.

Step Five: Admitted to God, to ourselves, and to another human being the exact nature of our wrongs.

Step Six: Were entirely ready to have God remove all these defects of character.

Step Seven: Humbly asked Him to remove our shortcomings.

Step Eight: Made a list of all persons we had harmed, and became willing to make amends to them all.

Step Nine: Made direct amends to such people wherever possible, except when to do so would injure them or others.

Step Ten: Continued to take personal inventory and when we were wrong promptly admitted it.

Alcoholics Anonymous is a program of spiritual development. Spiritual growth requires that we be honest with ourselves and with others about who we are and what we have done in our lives. We have to identify the behavior in our past that has injured others. We have to repair the damage that our past behavior has caused and then not behave that way again. Only then can we redeem ourselves. The word "redeem" means to set free from bondage, to rescue. It is through this process that we are released from the negative consequences of our past behavior and our character defects. We are set free.

The process of redemption takes place in Steps Four through Ten. It begins in Step Four when we take a moral inventory to identify our character defects. It continues in Step Five when we admit to ourselves, to God, and to another human being the exact nature of those defects. The pain of these two Steps makes us willing to have God remove our defects of character (Step Six). In Step Seven, we humbly ask God to do so. We become willing to make amends to those we have harmed in Step Eight. In Step Nine, we make the actual amends. But our redemption is not yet complete.

A complete amend includes *not repeating the same behavior.* Our amends mean nothing if we do not change the way we behave. Part of the way we make amends is to, literally, amend our behavior. If we do not change, our amends have been a sham, a temporary act without lasting effect. It is for that reason that Step Ten comes next: "Continued to take personal inventory and when we were wrong promptly admitted it." Step Ten keeps us from repeating the injuries of the past.

**We make amends for what
we have done, and we change
the way we behave.**

The Big Book says, "The spiritual life is not a theory. *We have to live it.*"[9] Living it is based on spiritual progress, not spiritual perfection. We make spiritual progress by working Steps Four through Nine once completely and by working Step Ten over and over again.

STEPS ELEVEN AND TWELVE

> *Step Eleven: Sought through prayer and meditation to improve our conscious contact with God* as we understood Him, *praying only for knowledge of His will for us and the power to carry that out.*
>
> *Step Twelve: Having had a spiritual awakening as the result of these steps, we tried to carry this message to alcoholics, and to practice these principles in all our affairs.*

In the Eleventh Step, we seek to improve our conscious contact with God through prayer and meditation. We pray *only* for knowledge of His will for us and the power to carry that out. The decision we made in the Third Step we now implement more fully.

Step Eleven outlines a regular program of daily prayer and meditation that begins in the morning, carries through the day whenever we are undecided or agitated, and ends in the evening. Prayer and meditation can take many forms. There may be as many forms of meditation in AA as there are concepts of a Higher Power. All that is required is that we earnestly try to determine our Higher Power's will for us that day and to bring our will into line with that Power's. In this way, we eliminate the "stinking thinking" that got us into such trouble, and we open ourselves to God, however we understand God. See chapter 6, "Say Your Prayers," for more on prayer and meditation.

**Step Eleven suggests
a daily program of
prayer and meditation.**

The Twelfth Step sums up AA's recovery program as a lifetime project of service to other alcoholics and the practice of spiritual principles. To work the Twelfth Step is to work all the other Steps as well.

Twelfth Step work means to carry the message of AA recovery to other alcoholics. AA was founded because Bill Wilson and Dr. Bob discovered that they needed to help other alcoholics in order to stay sober themselves. Twelfth Step work will be discussed more thoroughly in chapter 7, "Help Another Alcoholic."

**Steps Ten, Eleven, and Twelve
are sometimes called the
"maintenance Steps."**

Chapter 5

Call Your Sponsor

Sponsorship is one of the most powerful tools of Twelve Step recovery. A sponsor is another AA member who serves as a personal teacher, guide, listener, role model, and friend. Our sponsor helps us work the Twelve Steps; shares his or her personal experience, strength, and hope; and helps us stay on the recovery track. A sponsor is a crucial part of recovery.

**It is with a sponsor that we
work the Steps.**

Someone who is new to AA may begin with a "temporary sponsor." Many AA groups have lists of people who have volunteered to act as temporary or interim sponsors. A temporary sponsor serves the newcomer until a suitable long-term sponsor is found. Sometimes temporary sponsors become regular sponsors.

**We choose a temporary sponsor until
we can find a long-term one.**

Most of us who are new to AA have dozens of questions. A sponsor can help answer these questions no matter how dumb they seem to us. A sponsor can stay in daily contact to see how we're doing and lend a friendly ear to our concerns. It is through our sponsors that we begin to reestablish our trust in other human beings.

Generally, sponsors and sponsees are of the same sex. This custom prevents the intimacy that develops in the relationship from evolving into a romantic attachment that could jeopardize either person's recovery. In the case of heterosexual male/female sponsorships and homosexual same sex sponsorships, both the sponsor and the sponsee need to be aware of the risks involved. They both need to agree in advance that if friendship begins to turn into romance, the sponsor/sponsee relationship will be terminated.

Generally, sponsors and sponsees
should be of the same sex.

What do we look for in a sponsor? We may each look for something different, but there are some guidelines we should follow when selecting a sponsor. A sponsor should probably

1. Have at least one year of sobriety. This guideline is for the benefit of the potential sponsor as well as the sponsee. For the first year, it is a good idea for an AA member to stayed focused on his or her own sobriety.
2. Have a sponsor himself or herself.

Sponsors should have their own
sponsors. Our sponsor's sponsor
is called our "grand sponsor."

3. Realize the importance of the Steps and be willing to help us work them.
4. Have personally worked at least the first five Steps. If we get ahead of our sponsor in working the Steps, we need to find a new sponsor. AA is a program of action, not theory. A sponsor who has not worked a Step cannot help a sponsee work that Step. He or she has no experience, strength, and hope to share regarding the Step.

5. Promise to hold everything we say in strict confidence. There are two exceptions. One is the right to discuss us and our situation with our grand sponsor, but also in strict confidence. The other is when an unreported crime is confessed to a sponsor. Sponsors cannot offer the same legal confidentiality protection as ministers, lawyers, and doctors—they have a legal obligation to report certain crimes, especially if questioned by the police or a judge. If you confess a crime, be ready to face the consequences.

6. Be regularly available to us. Some sponsors ask their new sponsees to call them daily for the first thirty, sixty, or ninety days of sponsorship. Such regular contact helps our sponsor get to know us quicker and shows our commitment to the relationship.

**Sponsors need to be regularly
available to their sponsees.**

7. Emphasize that Alcoholics Anonymous is a program of honesty and insist that we be honest about what we are doing and where we are in our program. By the same token, our sponsor should agree to be honest with us.

8. Feel comfortable discussing the spiritual aspect of the program with us without imposing his or her religious beliefs or prejudices about a Higher Power.

9. Remind us that we are always free to find an additional sponsor or a replacement sponsor if the relationship doesn't work.

**Find a sponsor who
has what you want.**

How do we find a sponsor? The usual method is to listen in meetings for someone whose sharing is meaningful to us. Someone who regularly says things we can identify with and seems to have the kind of sobriety we want could be a good candidate. The goal is to find a sponsor who has what we want.

After identifying a potential sponsor, talk to this person about the possibility of sponsoring you. In the interview, try to determine whether or not the match is a good one. Do you have similar sponsorship goals? Do your personalities fit? Your potential sponsor is as interested as you are in a relationship that will work. Be honest about yourself and what you want.

The rewards of sponsorship are as great for the sponsor as for the sponsee.

Because so many of us fear rejection, it is often scary to ask someone to sponsor us. "What if they say 'no'?" we ask.

Well, if they say "no," they say "no."

But most AA members will not refuse to sponsor someone unless they have a good reason for doing so. For example, some may refuse because they travel too much, already sponsor as many people as they can handle, or will be moving away soon. It is generally agreed that the rewards of sponsoring are as great as the rewards of being sponsored. In fact, they may be greater. We pay people a high honor when we ask them to sponsor us. It is not a problem for them. On the contrary, it aids their spiritual growth and their program of recovery.

Don't let fear of rejection stand in the way of getting a sponsor.

Living Sober describes how the term "sponsor" came about:

> In the earliest days of A.A., the term "sponsor" was not in the A.A. jargon. Then a few hospitals in Akron, Ohio, and New York began to accept alcoholics (under that diagnosis) as patients—*if* a sober A.A. member would agree to "sponsor" the sick man or woman. The sponsor took the patient to the hospital, visited him or her regularly, was present when the patient was discharged, and took the patient home and then to an A.A. meeting. At the meeting, the sponsor introduced the newcomer to other happily nondrinking alcoholics. All through the early months of recovery, the sponsor stood by, ready to answer questions or to listen whenever needed.

Sponsorship turned out to be such a good way to help people get established in A.A. that it has become a custom followed throughout the A.A. world, even when hospitalization is not necessary.[1]

A slang word sometimes used in AA to mean sponsee is "pigeon." The term may also refer to someone new in the program. AA cofounder Dr. Bob probably coined the word. One AA member recalled that "Doc would often announce at a meeting, 'There's a pigeon in Room so-and-so who needs some attention.'"[2] According to Lois Wilson, Bill's wife, the use of the term "pigeon" came from AA's earliest days and was consistently used with great affection. In Akron and Cleveland, it was customary to call new members "babies," also used with a sense of affectionate care.[3]

Sponsees are sometimes called "pigeons" in AA.

Like any intimate relationship, the one between a sponsor and sponsee evolves over time. It may strengthen or weaken or never even get started. Sponsors are not forever (they die, too, after all). Some sponsors who serve us well in early sobriety are not as effective in later sobriety. Sponsors are also alcoholics and, like us, are only human. They lose their tempers, aren't always there when we need them, and may even relapse. When the relationship no longer works, find another sponsor.

In AA, we can change sponsors whenever we want.

Sponsorship only works for us when we use our sponsor. It is a good example of getting as much out of something as we put into it. Like the program itself, sponsorship works—if we work it!

Call your sponsor.

Chapter 6

Say Your Prayers

AA is a spiritual program. It is not a religious program in the sense of promoting specific beliefs about God. But it is a spiritual program in that it helps us establish a relationship with a Power greater than ourselves, however we choose to define that Power.

> **It has been said that religion is for those
> who want to avoid hell, whereas
> spirituality is for those who
> have already been there.**

The AA program was founded on the idea that a spiritual experience or a spiritual awakening is at the heart of the recovery process. The Big Book states that its "main object is to enable you to find a Power greater than yourself which will solve your problem."[1] AA uses the phrases "Higher Power" and "God as we understand Him" to describe that Power. Some AA members favor the term "God" while others prefer "Higher Power" or even "HP." It is sometimes said that at first all we need to know about God is that we are not God. Some newcomers use the AA group as their first higher power.

> **AA is a spiritual program that
> leads to a spiritual awakening.
> But it is not religious.**

Atheists and agnostics have found sobriety in AA along with Protestants, Catholics, Jews, Muslims, Buddhists, and members of many other religious denominations. AA does not ask us to change our religious beliefs, merely to clarify them.

THE TWELVE STEPS AND A SPIRITUAL AWAKENING

The purpose of the Twelve Steps is to bring about a spiritual awakening that will eliminate our obsession to drink. The Twelfth Step begins, "Having had a spiritual awakening as *the* result of these steps [italics added]. . . ." Dr. Carl Jung, one of the fathers of psychoanalysis, believed that only a vital spiritual experience could remove the compulsion to drink.[2]

> **The purpose of the Twelve Steps is to bring about a spiritual awakening.**

The terms "spiritual awakening" and "spiritual experience" are used throughout the Big Book. After the first edition was published, some AA members were confused about what the terms meant. Appendix 2 was added to the second edition to clarify their meaning. The Big Book calls a spiritual awakening and a spiritual experience personality changes, or religious experiences, that are "sufficient to bring about recovery from alcoholism." They may be in the nature of "sudden and spectacular upheavals." But most "develop slowly over a period of time. Quite often friends of the newcomer are aware of the difference long before he is. . . . With few exceptions our members find that they have tapped an unsuspected inner resource which they presently identify with their own conception of a Power greater than themselves.

Most of us think this awareness of a Power greater than ourselves is the essence of spiritual experience."[3]

> **An awareness of a Power greater than ourselves is the essence of spirituality.**

The difference between a spiritual awakening and a spiritual experience is simply timing: how long it takes. Bill Wilson had a spiritual experience in Towns Hospital that changed his life. Dr. Bob, who sought such an experience, instead had a spiritual awakening that changed his life.[4] The former occurred in a matter of minutes; the latter over a period of years. The Big Book states: "The great fact is just this, and nothing less: That we have had deep and effective spiritual experiences which have revolutionized our whole attitude toward life, toward our fellows and toward God's universe."[5]

Yet there are a lot of sober people in AA who will tell you that they have never had a spiritual awakening. Perhaps they have not. But it is clear that they have undergone significant changes in their lives. The words used to describe the change are not important, but the experience is.

PRAYER AND MEDITATION

AA suggests that we pray (or simply talk) to our Higher Power each morning. We ask our Higher Power to keep us sober that day, and that night we thank our Higher Power for doing so. It doesn't matter what our concept of the Higher Power is or to whom we pray as long as we pray. It has even been suggested that we simply pray "To whom it may concern."

> **We ask our Higher Power each
> morning to keep us sober.**

Of morning prayer and meditation, the Big Book says,

> On awakening let us think about the twenty-four hours ahead. We consider our plans for the day. Before we begin, we ask God to direct our thinking, especially asking that it be divorced from self-pity, dishonest or self-seeking motives. . . .
>
> . . . We usually conclude the period of meditation with a prayer that we be shown all through the day what our next step is to be, that we be given whatever we need to take care of such problems. We ask especially for freedom from self-will. . . . [6]

**A period of morning meditation
helps us begin the day
with a sense of serenity.**

The Big Book also suggests meditation at night:

> When we retire at night, we constructively review our day. Were we resentful, selfish, dishonest or afraid? Do we owe an apology? Have we kept something to ourselves which should be discussed with another person at once? Were we kind and loving toward all? What could we have done better? Were we thinking of ourselves most of the time? Or were we thinking of what we could do for others, of what we could pack into the stream of life?[7]

If we faithfully work the Twelve Steps, prayer and meditation will become part of our lives. AA's Eleventh Step calls for prayer and meditation as a way of improving our conscious contact with God *as we understand Him*. A handy distinction between prayer and meditation is this: prayer is speaking to our Higher Power whereas meditation is listening to that Power. The Rev. Samuel Shoemaker, one of Bill Wilson's spiritual advisors, said that a person must "grow up and stop just *using* God and begin to ask God to *use him*."[8] According to this Episcopal priest, "Real prayer is not telling God what we want. It is putting ourselves at His disposal so that He can tell us what He wants. Prayer is not trying to get God to change His will. It is trying to find out what His will is, to align ourselves or realign ourselves with His purpose for the world and for us."[9] Bill Wilson suggested that "when making specific requests, it will be well to add to each one of them this qualification: '. . . if it be Thy will.'"[10]

**Prayer is speaking to our Higher Power;
meditation is listening to that Power.**

Many who are new to the AA program have difficulty with prayer and meditation because of bad experiences with religion, because they have never used prayer or meditation before, or for other reasons.

Some newcomers don't believe in praying, but do it anyway. I have a good atheist friend in AA who has been sober for over a decade. He says he "doesn't believe in the effectiveness of prayer, but it works." So he prays, especially when he's hurting. Bill Wilson wrote, "It has been well said that 'almost the only scoffers at prayer are those who never tried it enough.'"[11]

There are a lot of Twelve Step and other meditation books that AA members find helpful. And there are many ways to meditate. What is important is to find a method that works. Meditation is a tool to discover our Higher Power's will and to abandon the self-will that has brought us unhappiness. It is a way of changing our attitudes and perceptions, and it brings us into closer contact with our Higher Power.

**We claim spiritual progress
rather than spiritual perfection.**

Chapter 7

Help Another Alcoholic

Bill Wilson and Dr. Bob discovered that the key to maintaining sobriety is to help another alcoholic. The Big Book states, "Practical experience shows that nothing will so much insure immunity from drinking as intensive work with other alcoholics. It works when other activities fail."[1]

Helping another alcoholic is called Twelfth Step work, because the suggestion to do so appears in the Twelfth Step. An AA expression that explains Twelfth Step work is "You have to give it away in order to keep it." Twelfth Step work includes sharing our experience, strength, and hope with others both in meetings and outside meetings. And it includes sponsorship and service work of all kinds, from chairing meetings to making coffee. Helping other alcoholics keeps us in touch with our own vulnerability to alcohol and leads us out of our self-absorption. Self-pity, in particular, seems to leave in the face of another person's problems. Working with newcomers renews our recovery, keeps it "green" for us. Newcomers remind us of what it was like in the last days of our own drinking.

**Working with another alcoholic
is called Twelfth Step work.**

Alcoholism has been described as the "disease of loneliness." But working with others relieves our sense of isolation and the feeling that we are "terminally unique." We discover that we are like others and that we have more in common than we had suspected. We feel less afraid and more in tune with the world when we connect with another alcoholic and try to help him or her stay sober. As is often said in AA, "Alcoholics Anonymous is a 'we' program."

Working with others relieves our sense of isolation and our loneliness.

Working with other alcoholics has another advantage. When we work with a newcomer, we teach by words and example. We share our experience, strength, and hope regarding AA, and we model recovery. In the process of teaching others what we have learned, we teach ourselves. Many times as a sponsor I have changed my own behavior because of something I had said to a sponsee. So my experience has confirmed the old saying "Teachers learn more than their students." It is a blessing to be a teacher. In AA, we are all teachers, and we are all students.

Helping another alcoholic is one of the ways we stay sober.

When our work takes us to the still-suffering alcoholic, it is called a "Twelfth Step call." In the days before AA was well known, before judges sent people with DWIs to AA, and before alcoholism treatment centers funneled thousands of people into the program, word of mouth was the primary source of new members. An alcoholic was most likely to learn about AA through a friend who knew someone in the program. All that the friend knew about AA was that it might be able to help. As a result, there were more classic Twelfth Step calls in the old days. Often the call was made on someone who was still drinking. Chapter 7 in the Big Book, "Working with Others," is devoted entirely to Twelfth Step calls and how to make them.

About sobriety, it is said in AA that in order to keep it, you have to give it away.

Such calls still happen. When someone telephones AA for the first time and wants to speak to someone about his or her alcoholism, the person responding on the phone is making a Twelfth Step call. So are the people who later visit the suffering alcoholic to share their experience, strength, and hope. Sometimes the suffering alcoholic is a "wet drunk" (still drinking) and sometimes he or she is "dry" for the moment. Either way, AA tradition suggests that, for safety's sake, a classic Twelfth Step call be made with two AA members present. Never make a Twelfth Step call alone unless you know the person well and he or she is sober.

**Twelfth Step calls on strangers
should be made in pairs.**

Many newcomers are bitterly disappointed when the person they have Twelfth-Stepped fails to get sober or quickly relapses. The Big Book tells us that our only purpose is to carry the message. It is not our job to get the alcoholic sober. Whether or not a drinking alcoholic gets sober is up to that person and God. We do our part by bringing the message of recovery, but we have to leave the results to our Higher Power.

**We carry the message. We do
not get an alcoholic sober.**

Many Twelfth Step calls result in a new AA member. But many calls bear no fruit or only bear fruit many months or even years later. We make Twelfth Step calls to help the suffering alcoholic, but we make them for ourselves as well. It is one of the ways we stay sober. Regardless of whether or not the new person finds sobriety, our Twelfth Step call has been a success if we did not drink that day.

**Our Twelfth Step call has been
successful if we did not drink that day.**

Chapter 8

Put Sobriety First

As alcoholics in recovery, maintaining sobriety is our first priority. Especially in the early days, sobriety seems to require a lot of sacrifices. We give up old habits, attitudes, perceptions, even friends. We spend time attending AA meetings, talking with our sponsors, reading the Big Book. All these changes require effort and sometimes inconvenience. This time of so much change can be scary and lonely and anger-producing. But it is necessary if we want to stay sober.

**Sobriety is our
highest priority.**

Sobriety has to be number one for us. If it isn't, we may be distracted by whatever *is* number one. When our jobs, our old friends, our hobbies, or our favorite television shows become more important than the work of sobriety, we are in trouble. The experience of millions of alcoholics in recovery proves the necessity of putting our sobriety above everything else. The old sports analogy still applies: we have to keep our eyes on the ball if we want to win the game.

I have known of misguided husbands and wives who offered their alcoholic spouses a choice between their marriage and "all those meetings." The spouses who quite wisely chose the meetings stayed sober. Had they stopped going to AA and returned to drinking, they probably would have lost their spouses anyway when they lost their sobriety. Our daily choices between AA and competing activities are usually not so dramatic. But we still have to make choices as we change the priorities of our life and put sobriety first. As the Big Book says, "We all had to place recovery above everything. . . ."[1]

Our sobriety cannot depend upon any factor outside ourselves. It cannot depend on how life treats us, on what others think, on how well we do financially, on whether or not we find a spouse. It cannot depend on anything except our desire to stay sober for ourselves. It cannot depend on our family's desire for us to stay sober. Nor on our boss' hopes for us. It can only depend on us. We cannot say, "I'll stay sober if only such-and-such happens" and stay sober.

The Big Book captures this idea of putting sobriety first in the phrase "willing to go to any length to get it."[2] Putting sobriety first is, therefore, about willingness. It is also about acceptance: accepting that, as alcoholics, we cannot drink normally (or use other mood-altering chemicals). And it is about change: doing whatever we have to do to stay sober instead of whatever we want to do.

**We became willing to go to
any length to stay sober.**

Whenever we are faced with a difficult decision, we ask ourselves, "How will this decision affect my sobriety?" Any action that will endanger our sobriety must be abandoned or avoided. No matter what.

**S.L.I.P.—Sobriety
Loses Its Priority.**

"Sobriety first" becomes the North Star for us. We will never lose our way if we follow that guide.

Put sobriety first.

Chapter 9

Take Sobriety and Life
One Day at a Time

Taking life and sobriety "One day at a time" is perhaps the most powerful of all AA strategies. It is such a profound concept for living that it enriches the lives of all who practice it, alcoholic or not. But for the alcoholic, it has special meaning. At the most basic level, one day at a time means that we do not decide to quit drinking for a week, a month, a year, or a lifetime. We simply choose not to drink for the next twenty-four-hour period. If that time period is too long, then we choose not to drink for the next twelve hours, or the next hour, or the next ten minutes. We break the seemingly infinite future into manageable periods of time.

**AA members quit drinking
for one day at a time, not for
the rest of their lives.**

None of us can say that he or she will never drink again. But each of us can choose not to drink *today*. We may not know about tomorrow, but we don't have to know about tomorrow. We only have to know about today. Although we may count our sobriety in years, we measure our sobriety in days. It is more accurate to say we have been sober for 365 days than to say we have been sober for one year. Even the oldest old-timer still takes it one day at a time.

In addition to taking sobriety one day at a time, we learn in AA to take life one day at a time. The application of this principle keeps us centered in the present moment where life is actually occurring. It wards off fear of the future as well as regret for the past. One day at a time helps us get through periods of great difficulty or stress, which we only have to stand for one day. And it also focuses our joy during periods of great happiness by keeping us in the present where we can fully experience it.

**One day at a time keeps us
from fearing the future
or regretting the past.**

Bill Wilson is credited with using the phrase "one day at a time" when he returned to New York City after his first meeting with Dr. Bob.[1] Apparently, he and Dr. Bob "had stumbled across the phrase [twenty-four hours at a time] almost by accident while working with new men who were still drinking. Neither of them would ask a drunk if he wanted to stop forever. They knew that the vision of a world stretching on with no booze ad infinitum was impossible for any drinker to contemplate, so they asked if he thought he could stop for one day. All men at some time or other had been dry for a day. And if this seemed too rough a proposition, they would bring it down to just one hour."[2]

**We make no promises
for the future.
We just stay sober today.**

Chapter 10

Use the Serenity Prayer

The Serenity Prayer is a powerful tool for finding peace and balance when events and emotions threaten to overwhelm us. When we are frightened, angry, impatient, lonely, or tempted to drink, repeating its words has a soothing effect. The single-sentence prayer contains six key AA concepts: God (or Higher Power), serenity, acceptance, change, courage, and wisdom. Its unique calming power lies in the central life issue that it reminds us to consider: the distinction between what we can and cannot change.

God, grant me the serenity
to accept the things I cannot change,
the courage to change the things I can,
and the wisdom to know the difference.

In our drinking days, we wasted time and energy trying to change the things we could not change while refusing to change the things we could. As a result, we complained about what life did to us instead of taking responsibility for doing something about our problems. We whined, but we would not act. Or else we took on impossible tasks.

In every situation where we have lost our serenity, the Serenity Prayer leads us to ask ourselves what is possible for us to change about the situation and what is impossible for us to change. If we are trying to change the impossible, we need to practice acceptance instead. If there is something in the situation that we can change but are ignoring, we need to go ahead and change it. Usually, what we need to change is ourselves. There isn't much else in life we have control over.

**God, grant me the serenity
to accept the things I cannot change.**

The beginning of the Serenity Prayer reminds us that the serenity we seek comes from a Higher Power. It is to this Higher Power that we turn in the prayer. We ask God, as we understand Him, to provide the serenity we need to accept the things we cannot change, the courage to change the things we can, and the wisdom to know which is which. Serenity can come from acceptance or from action, depending upon whether something can or cannot be changed.

So much of AA's recovery program is captured by the Serenity Prayer that some think it began as an AA prayer. It did not. Bill Wilson tells the story of how the prayer came to be adopted by the Fellowship in early 1942.

> . . . A news clipping whose content was to become famous was called to our attention by a New York member, newsman Jack. It was an obituary notice from a New York paper. Underneath a routine account of the one who had died there appeared . . . [the words of the Serenity Prayer].
>
> Never had we seen so much A.A. in so few words. While Ruth [Bill's secretary] and I were admiring the prayer, and wondering how to use it, friend Howard walked into the office. Confirming our own ideas, he exclaimed, "We ought to print this on cards and drop one into every piece of mail that goes out of here. I'll pay for the first printing." For several years afterward we followed his suggestion, and with amazing speed the Serenity Prayer came into general use. . . . [1]

**God, grant me the courage
to change the things I can.**

Although no one knows for sure who wrote the Serenity Prayer, "it is usually credited to Reinhold Niebuhr, a 20th-century theologian, who in turn credited an 18th-century theologian, Friedrich Oetinger."[2] Dr. Niebuhr wrote down the prayer in 1932 in substantially the same form as we know it in AA. It was his opinion that the prayer might have been around for centuries.[3]

Use the Serenity Prayer.

Chapter 11

Remember: It's the First Drink
That Gets Us Drunk

The first drink sets up the alcoholic craving that leads to the second drink and the third and the fourth and so on. Therefore, it is the *first* drink—not the last drink—that gets us drunk. As they say in AA, "When you're run over by a train, it's the engine that kills you, not the caboose."

> **It may be the last drink that gets the
> normal drinker drunk, but *it's the first
> drink that gets an alcoholic drunk.***

One of the primary symptoms of alcoholism is impaired control, meaning that alcoholics cannot guarantee their behavior after their first drink. Sometimes they can control whether or not they have another drink and sometimes they can't. Ultimately, they will lose control and drink too many. The only way to stop this process of one-drink-after-another is to avoid drinking any alcohol. Not drinking any alcohol is called "abstinence." Abstinence is the only treatment for alcoholism. There is no cure.

According to the American Medical Association, alcohol "has a psychological effect that modifies thinking and reasoning. One drink can change the thinking of an alcoholic so that he feels he can tolerate another, and then another, and another. . . ."[1]

**It's the first drink that leads us to the
second, the third, the fourth, and so on.**

It is easy to be seduced by the old thinking that whispers, "I'll just have one drink." As if any of us alcoholics ever wanted "just one drink." It is precisely that one drink, *that very first drink,* that leads, finally, to complete loss of control. "It's the first drink that gets us drunk" counters the old idea that we can somehow control our drinking *this time.* When we understand that alcoholism is a disease and that the first drink activates that disease, we can appreciate why no amount of alcohol is safe for us.

Alcoholism has nothing to do with willpower. All the willpower in the world will not protect us once we have taken the first drink. We can use the AA program to help us not take that first drink. But once we have taken it, not even AA can help us until we stop drinking and start over again.

The phrase, "It's the first drink that gets us drunk" may have come from one of Dr. Bob's expressions from AA's earliest days. Warned the cofounder, "The first one will get you."[2]

It's the first drink that gets you.

What is true of alcohol for the alcoholic is also true of other drugs for the drug addict. It is the first hit that gets us high, not the last. Like alcoholics, we cannot control our use of mind-altering chemicals after the first hit, pill, or injection.

Chapter 12

Think the Drink Through

"Think the drink through" is a tool that helps us when we are tempted to drink. It means to think about what would happen to us if we were to take that drink. We are alcoholics. We know the first drink would activate our craving for alcohol. It would drive us to other drinks and ultimately to the last drink, and it would bring on the negative consequences that accompany our active alcoholism.

When we have a pleasant thought about drinking, we remind ourselves that drinking is no longer an option for us. When we think something like, "Wouldn't a beer taste good!" we acknowledge that, yes, it might. But we also remind ourselves that *a* beer isn't something that we've wanted for a long time. *A case* of beer, maybe, or perhaps *a couple of six-packs,* but not *a* beer. *A* beer is for normal drinkers, not for alcoholics.

**When we "think the drink through,"
we remember that it's the first
drink that gets us drunk.**

When we are tempted to drink, we remind ourselves of our last drunk. We remember how we couldn't control our drinking and what it felt like the first day we came into AA. "Is that something I want to experience again?" we ask ourselves. We think the drink through. We say to ourselves, "If I have the first drink, I will want another and another. I will get drunk. If not today, then tomorrow or the next day.

The old craving will come back. And all the pain. Bad things will happen to me again as they did in the last days of my drinking. And I will regret it."

**It helps to remember our last drunk
when we are tempted to drink.**

We think the drink through because we never know what the cost of that first drink might be. For some, it has been the loss of a job. For others, it has been another DWI and jail time. For still others, the price has been their lives. Whatever happiness or escape alcohol may once have brought us is now too costly.

The Big Book story entitled "The Man Who Mastered Fear" describes another way to think the drink through. Its author writes, "There have also been numerous times when I have thought about taking a drink. Such thinking usually began with thoughts of the pleasant drinking of my youth. I learned early in my A.A. life that I could not afford to fondle such thoughts, as you might fondle a pet, because this particular pet could grow into a monster. Instead, I quickly substitute one or another vivid scene from the nightmare of my later drinking."[1]

**Alcohol is no longer a pleasant release
for us—it's a dangerous drug.**

Chapter 13

Avoid Slippery Places

To "slip" is to drink again after a period of sobriety. "Slippery places" refer to actual places or to emotional states and situations in which we are more likely to drink again. A slippery place is anywhere a special temptation to drink exists because of old habits, friends, memories, pressures, emotions, or the availability of alcohol. Bars that we used to frequent can be slippery places, but so can hanging out with old drinking buddies who still drink. For other drugs, a slippery place is any place associated with using, such as your dealer's or an old using buddy's house, or any situation that normally went along with using, such as a certain kind of music.

**To "slip" is to drink after
a period of sobriety.**

A slippery place can also be a state of mind. When we are hungry, angry, lonely, or tired, we are more vulnerable to drinking or using. So, we are reminded to avoid H.A.L.T. (getting too hungry, angry, lonely, or tired). Resentments pose special traps for the recovering alcoholic. In a fit of rage, many of us have "drunk at" somebody else only to hurt ourselves instead. So we monitor our H.A.L.T., our resentments, and our spiritual program when deciding whether a place, event, situation, or circumstance is slippery for us.

**A slippery place can be a bar,
a group of old drinking friends,
or a state of mind.**

We cannot avoid alcohol entirely in the real world, nor do we have to. The Big Book assures us that "assuming we are spiritually fit, we can do all sorts of things alcoholics are not supposed to do."[1] We don't have to live in fear of alcohol, although we do have to respect its power over us. Part of respecting that power is avoiding places or situations that are likely to lead us back to drinking. Within that restriction, however, we can lead normal lives.

Part 4 of this book, "The Survival Guide," contains many practical suggestions for staying sober in places that are potentially slippery. We have to avoid some places entirely. But we can make other places less slippery by following guidelines that AA members have developed over the years. The Big Book says, "So our rule is not to avoid a place where there is drinking, *if we have a legitimate reason for being there.*"[2] A legitimate reason for being there is the key. It may be okay to go to a bar if a business meeting has been scheduled there, but it is not okay if we are alone and feeling edgy.

**As alcoholics in recovery,
we can go wherever we want to go
as long as we have a *legitimate*
reason for being there.**

In the end, we have to define our own slippery places. What is slippery for one person may not be slippery for another, which is why we need to be honest with ourselves and why we need sponsors. If a place feels slippery, stay away. Alcohol is cunning, baffling, and powerful. It is always better to be safe than sorry where alcohol or any other drug is concerned.

Avoid slippery places.

Chapter 14

Use AA Slogans

AA slogans help us stay focused on AA principles. They remind us of attitudes and actions that will strengthen our recovery, and they lead us to productive behavior. Dozens of AA slogans and expressions have evolved over the years. Some are original with AA, and some are not.

Most AA expressions come from the Big Book, the Twelve and Twelve, or tradition. "Keep coming back," for example, seems to have started with Dr. Bob's wife. "Progress not perfection" came from the Big Book. As time passes, new sayings are adopted and old sayings are abandoned. "Take the cotton out of your ears and put it in your mouth" is not used as often as it used to be. On the other hand, "It works if you work it" began in the 1980s.

**AA slogans help us
focus on AA principles.**

The following expressions are among those that you will hear regularly in AA.

ACCEPT LIFE ON LIFE'S TERMS

The restoration to sanity that the Second Step talks about refers to living in reality instead of the fantasies we favored as drinking alcoholics. Reality is "life's terms." When we accept life on life's terms, we deal with reality. When we refuse to accept the way life is, we return to fantasy. Most of us wish that life were different in some way. We want it to be easier, less painful, more certain. As long as we object to life's terms and fight them, trying *to change life* instead of ourselves, we will not be happy. Life is the way life is. But *we* are changeable. It is only when we embrace life with all its problems that we are able to view it differently. By changing our attitudes and perceptions, we can change the way we see life and, thus, the way life is for us.

**Accepting reality is
accepting "life's terms."**

Easy Does It . . . But Do It

In early recovery, it is easy to be frantic about life. We worry about the changes we have to make, the things we have to do, and the past we have to face. The expression "Easy does it" reminds us to take it easy, relax, calm down. It's one step at a time. We don't have to do everything at once. And sometimes we shouldn't do anything at all. Life occasionally calls for inaction. In sobriety, we learn to pace ourselves and to take life and sobriety one day at a time.

"But do it" is often added to the slogan to remind us that "Easy does it" is not an excuse for putting things off. We still have responsibilities to meet. Nor is "Easy does it" an excuse for hoping someone else will do for us what we should do for ourselves.

**"Easy does it" is not an
excuse for putting things off.**

Keep Coming Back

In a narrow sense, the expression "Keep coming back" means to keep coming back to AA meetings and life will get better. In a broader sense, the expression means to keep coming back to AA principles. AA is a design for living that works. If we keep coming back to the principles of the program, we'll be able to overcome life's problems as they arise. More than that, we'll find serenity and joy. The challenge is to keep coming back to meetings and principles when we aren't getting what we want as well as when life is so great that we don't think we need to.

**Keep coming back to AA
meetings and AA principles.**

KEEP IT SIMPLE

AA has been described as a simple program for complex people. As alcoholics, our tendency is to complicate things and then be overwhelmed by them. "Keep it simple" reminds us not to complicate matters. It is easy to be distracted by unimportant issues when we need to focus on what is important: Staying sober.

Here are some examples of keeping it simple: Don't drink, go to meetings, read the Big Book, work the Steps, call your sponsor, say your prayers, and do the next right thing. The acronym often used for "Keep it simple" is K.I.S.S. (Keep it simple, stupid).

K.I.S.S. helps us resist over-analysis as a defense against action. It keeps us from complaining that we don't know what to do when we know but don't want to do it. K.I.S.S. also means that we don't have to solve all our problems at once. It keeps us from being overwhelmed by both the real and imagined complexities of life. We can take our problems one at a time, one day at a time.

"Keep it simple" was Dr. Bob's favorite expression.[1] It was his last piece of advice to Bill Wilson before Bill returned to New York City after their first meeting in 1935.[2] "Keep it simple" were also Dr. Bob's last words to Bill Wilson before Dr. Bob died in 1950.[3] And Dr. Bob's last caution to Alcoholics Anonymous was, "Let's not louse this thing up; let's keep it simple."[4]

**Dr. Bob's last words to Bill Wilson
were "Keep it simple."**

LET GO AND LET GOD

When we have done all that we can do, we ask our Higher Power to do the rest. We let go and let God. Some things cannot be accomplished by human power alone. We need a Power greater than ourselves to help us. Staying sober is one example of something we can't do by ourselves. Removing our character defects is another. Many times in our lives we are asked to perform beyond our capability. When that happens, we let go of the problem and let God solve it.

**God can do for us what we
cannot do for ourselves.**

The expression "Let go and let God" also means that when we are concerned about the outcome of a situation, we let go of the result and let God decide what will happen. We are expected to do the footwork, but the outcome of our labor is not ours to determine. Whatever happens is up to God, not to us. To let go and let God is to say to our Higher Power, "I've done all I can. I know the outcome I want in this situation, but the results are up to you. Your will, not mine, be done."

LIVE AND LET LIVE

It is often less painful to concern ourselves with other people's lives than it is to focus on our own. It is also easier to blame others than to accept responsibility for what happens to us. In recovery, we try to concentrate on our own character defects rather than on those of others. We practice tolerance by acknowledging our shortcomings and permitting others to have their own. Our need to criticize other people's behavior becomes less important than our need to respect them as individuals. We give them the right to make their own decisions, and we try not to judge them when we have not walked in their shoes.

**Tolerance means focusing on our similarities
to others rather than on our differences.**

PROGRESS, NOT PERFECTION

Our goal is to make progress—not to achieve perfection—in our

AA program and in our lives. When we try to do things perfectly, we are trying to do the impossible. Perfectionism is a reflection of alcoholic grandiosity. It is a God-like position of having to *be* right and *do* right at all times. It allows us to forgive others for their mistakes, but not to forgive ourselves.

Perfectionism stops us from really living. It keeps us from acting because we know we can't live up to our impossible standards. Or it throws us into pain and remorse for imagined failures when we do act. Perfectionism stands in the way of maturity, emotional balance, and spiritual growth. It is the enemy of change. Bill Wilson wrote, "We are all perfectionists who, failing perfection, have gone to the other extreme and settled for the bottle and the blackout."[5]

"Progress not perfection"
is a goal, not an excuse
for inaction.

THIS, TOO, SHALL PASS

Everything in life is temporary. Change is the only thing that's permanent. Every moment is unique, and we will never experience it again. Nothing recurs with precisely the same combination of age, experience, knowledge, attitude, and circumstance. The expression "This, too, shall pass" is a call for living in the moment and enjoying its uniqueness to the fullest. The best times of our lives, like the worst, don't last forever.

Just as the expression urges us to enjoy the happy times, it also reassures us in the difficult times. It reminds us not to let momentary setbacks, pain, or crises keep us from staying sober. No matter how painful or frightening events or emotions may be, they will eventually pass and time will heal them. We will survive—*if* we don't drink. What we have to do is get through the painful times with our sobriety intact. This expression can help us do it.

Bad times don't last forever.

Turn It Over

In Step Three, we "Made a decision to turn our will and our lives over to the care of God *as we understand Him.*" To turn our will and our lives over to God's care means to ask for God's guidance and to accept God's will for us. Alcoholics are usually preoccupied with control. We want to control the events of our lives, other people, the results of our efforts. In our drinking days, we believed we had such control. In sobriety, we realize that we didn't have control. We learn that we can make choices about what *we* do and little else. The slogan "Turn it over" reminds us to give up the control we never had and turn it over to our Higher Power instead.

Newcomers sometimes get confused about this phrase and think that it means turning everything over to God, including all the work that has to be done! We still do the footwork to achieve our goals, but we turn the results of that footwork over to God. We give up the idea that we are in control of the *outcome* of our efforts. For example, if we need a job, we have to do the footwork: read the want ads, write the resumes, fill out the applications, call potential employers, make contacts with people we know, and so on. It is only the *result*—the job we get or don't get—that we turn over. We do not turn over the hard work!

**We turn over to God the results of our
efforts, not the efforts themselves
which we are still expected to make.**

Other common slogans and phrases you're likely to hear in AA include the following:

Easing God Out (E.G.O.)

When we ease God as we understand Him out of our decisions and make decisions only on the basis of our ego or self-will, we are heading for trouble.

GO WITH THE FLOW

When we go with the flow, we practice acceptance and bring our will in line with our Higher Power's.

PEOPLE, PLACES, AND THINGS

Before recovery, we depended on people, places, or things to make us happy—or blamed them for our problems. In recovery, we learn that we cannot change external events; we can only change ourselves.

PRINCIPLES BEFORE PERSONALITIES

It is the principles of the program, not its personalities, that guide recovery and keep us sober.

STICK WITH THE WINNERS

In choosing friends in AA, we pick those whose sobriety we admire.

PART 2

AA MEETINGS AND GROUPS

Chapter 15

AA Groups

There are more than eighty thousand AA groups in America.[1] Some groups have only one meeting a week. Other groups have thirty-five or more. Wherever we travel in the United States, we'll usually find an AA meeting to attend.

THE FIRST AA GROUPS

The Big Book dates the founding of the first AA group from the moment AA's third member, Bill D., left the hospital to meet with Bill Wilson and Dr. Bob in Akron, Ohio. That date was June 13 or June 14, 1935.[2] Akron Group Number One was the first AA group in the world. Bill Wilson started AA Group Number Two in New York City.

> **The first AA group was founded in
> June 1935 when Bill Wilson and
> Dr. Bob met with Bill D.**

The first AA meetings in Akron and New York City were held as part of Oxford Group meetings. The Oxford Group was a nondenominational spiritual movement that met in small groups and tried to practice basic Christian principles. These first AA meetings were attended by recovering alcoholics, their spouses, other family members, good friends, and Oxford Group members. Later, when AA separated from the Oxford Group, its meetings were restricted to AA members and their families.[3] In the beginning, the meetings were usually held in homes and were open.[4]

By late 1937 private, or closed, meetings had begun to be held upstairs at the Wilson's home after the regular, or open, meeting downstairs. The private meetings were attended by Bill Wilson and other alcoholics who wished to ask confidential questions about alcoholism. Such closed meetings made possible a basic ingredient of recovery: honest sharing. The spouses and other family members remained downstairs.[5]

HOW TO BECOME AN AA GROUP MEMBER

There is no application process for admission to any AA group. As AA's Third Tradition states, "The only requirement for A.A. membership is a desire to stop drinking." Bill Wilson describes what this Tradition means, ". . . A.A. is really saying to every serious drinker, 'You are an A.A. member if *you* say so. You can declare yourself in; nobody can keep you out. No matter who you are, no matter how low you've gone, no matter how grave your emotional complications— even your crimes—we still can't deny you A.A. We don't *want* to keep you out. We aren't a bit afraid you'll harm us, never mind how twisted or violent you may be. We just want to be sure that you get the same great chance for sobriety that we've had. So you're an A.A. member the minute you declare yourself.'"[6] As long as we are alcoholics and do not disrupt a meeting, we are technically welcome at any AA meeting in the world.

**All alcoholics are
welcome in AA.**

HOME GROUP

Most AA members have a "home group," a group meeting which they regularly attend and call "home." The members of this group often seem like an extended family. They come to know us well in our sobriety. Regular attendance at a home group builds a strong foundation that provides continuing support for our recovery. It is in the home group that we express our opinions through group conscience meetings (see below) and answer the call to service. The home group is the strongest link we have to the Fellowship.[7]

A "home group" is an AA group we regularly attend and call "home."

GROUP OFFICERS

Tradition Two states, "Our leaders are but trusted servants; they do not govern." AA groups generally have the following officers: chairperson or secretary who chooses the meeting leader, treasurer, literature chairperson, General Service Representative, and Intergroup (Central Office) representative. Larger or better-organized groups may also have these officers: Grapevine representative, treatment facilities representative, public information representative, and correctional facilities representative.

According to AA's Second Tradition, "Our leaders are but trusted servants; they do not govern."

It is traditional within AA to rotate officers on a three-month, six-month, or, occasionally, a twelve-month basis. Rotations encourage humility, allow more individuals to serve, and fulfill the tradition of principles before personalities.

GROUP CONSCIENCE

AA's Second Tradition states, "For our group purpose there is but one ultimate authority—a loving God as He may express Himself in our group conscience." In practice, the "group conscience" is a process that each AA group uses to make decisions that affect the group as a whole, such as meeting format and the election of officers. Group conscience meetings are held before or after regular AA meetings. Every member of the group is entitled to vote.

Before the group votes, all information important to the decision is studied and time is taken to hear every view on that subject. In this way the group decision is based on an "informed group conscience"[8] that is more than a majority vote. It is a process that is designed to protect the group from a majority that is in error. The AA pamphlet *The A.A. Group* clarifies how the process works.

> **Through its "group conscience,"**
> **an AA group makes decisions on**
> **matters that affect it as a whole.**

Group Names

Each AA group has its own name which is related in some way to AA, alcoholism, recovery, or the group's location. Groups avoid names that imply an affiliation with, or an endorsement of, any venture outside AA. For example, "Presbyterian Hospital Group" suggests that AA is associated with Presbyterian Hospital, and so it is not acceptable. Some examples of AA group names are Zoo Group, River Oakes, West Side, Serenity, New Beginnings, Came to Believe, Saturday Night Live, Big Book, and Just for Today.

> **Each AA group**
> **has its own name.**

Service in Groups

Service is AA's Third Legacy. The Big Book states, "Our real purpose is to fit ourselves to be of maximum service to God and the people about us."[9] According to custom, AA members agree to serve when asked to do so unless they have a good reason not to. Service breaks through our tendency as alcoholics to isolate ourselves and become obsessed with our own problems. It encourages us to make new friends in AA and helps us feel more a part of the group. Service is also a way of paying back some of what we have been given. The AA Fellowship is a volunteer program. Without volunteers, it cannot function.

**It is customary to say "yes" when
asked to serve in AA unless there is
a good reason to say "no."**

There are many ways to serve within AA besides being a group officer. Here are some of the ways we serve:

1. Chairing or leading a meeting
2. Being a meeting speaker
3. Sharing our experience, strength, and hope when called upon in a meeting or by volunteering
4. Giving our name and telephone number to newcomers
5. Being a temporary or permanent sponsor
6. Making Twelfth Step calls (with another person)
7. Volunteering to answer the Intergroup/Central Office telephones
8. Setting up a meeting and cleaning up afterward.

Service is gratitude in action.

AA CLUBS

An AA club is a meeting place used exclusively by AA groups. Since owning or managing real estate is against the Twelve Traditions, there is technically no such thing as an AA club. AA groups do not own or run the clubs. Clubs are managed by nonprofit corporations formed by AA members acting as private individuals and not as AA members. These corporations then rent the meeting facilities (the clubs) to AA groups.

**AA clubs are not owned or run by
AA groups. They are separate facilities
rented to AA groups for meetings.**

A clubhouse provides a place for AA members to get together anytime during the hours it is open. Some clubs provide food and a variety of nonalcoholic drinks, lounges, rooms for cards and other games, large and small meeting rooms, and private rooms for conferences with sponsors. Clubs range from the run-down to elegant, and some are open twenty-four hours a day, every day of the year. AA's first clubhouse opened at 334 1/2 West 24th Street, New York City, in February 1940.

Many clubs have members who pay monthly dues in order to help cover the expenses of the club house. In some clubs, a membership is required to use part of the facilities (such as the card room). However, *all AA meetings* are open to *all AA members,* even those who are not members of the club. As long as you're an AA member, you're welcome in any AA club and all the meetings held there.

Chapter 16

AA Meetings

This chapter covers the history, purpose, and format of AA meetings. Read the chapter all the way through or pick the topics that interest you the most.

THE FIRST AA MEETING (1935)

The first meeting of the cofounders of Alcoholics Anonymous took place in Akron, Ohio, on Mother's Day (May 12th), 1935.[1] Visiting in Akron, Bill Wilson had looked for another alcoholic to work with in order to stay sober. That alcoholic turned out to be Dr. Bob. Although the cofounders met in May, Dr. Bob drank again. The official date of AA's founding is June 10, 1935, the day of Dr. Bob's last drink.

**AA was founded on
June 10, 1935.**

TYPES OF MEETINGS

AA meetings can be categorized in several different ways. The following classifications are the most common:

Closed or Open

Closed meetings: Meetings only for alcoholics and for those who think they might have a problem with alcohol. Nonalcoholics are asked not to attend.

Closed AA meetings are for alcoholics only or for those who think they might have a problem with their drinking.

Open meetings: Meetings for alcoholics as well as for their family, friends, and other interested parties (e.g., clergy, medical students).

Subject Matter

Speaker meetings: Meetings in which one or two AA members tell what their drinking was like before AA, what brought them into AA, and what their life is like now.

Discussion meetings: Meetings in which a topic suggested by the leader or someone is discussed by the members.

Big Book study: The Big Book is read and discussed in these meetings.

Step study: Meetings in which the Twelve Steps are read and discussed, usually at the rate of one Step per meeting.

Twelve and Twelve: Meetings in which the *Twelve Steps and Twelve Traditions* is read and discussed, usually at the rate of one chapter per meeting.

Tradition meetings: The Twelve Traditions are read and discussed in these meetings.

Beginners meetings: These meetings are primarily for beginners and usually focus on the first three Steps or serve as question-and-answer sessions. The meetings are generally chaired by someone who has a solid period of sobriety. (A "Guide for Leading Beginners Meetings" is available from AA's General Service Office.)

Ask-it basket: A basket with paper and pencils is passed around at the beginning of these meetings. Those who have questions or topics they would liked discussed write them on the paper. The leader draws the topics/questions from the basket and each is discussed as long as time permits.

**AA meetings come in a variety of
forms: speaker, discussion, Step study,
beginners, Tradition study, Big Book,
ask-it basket, and so on.**

Group Conscience Meetings

These meetings are held after regular AA meetings to make decisions that affect the entire group (such as election of officers). See "Group Conscience" in chapter 15, "AA Groups."

Business Meetings

These meetings provide an opportunity for group officers to report on group finances and activities. They are usually held after regular AA meetings, and voting is restricted to group members.

Group Inventory Meetings

These meetings are held periodically to evaluate how well the group is fulfilling its primary purpose of helping alcoholics recover through AA's Twelve Step program.

Special Interest Meetings

These meetings for people with a common interest besides alcoholism are held in most large cities. These group members find that their recovery is enriched when they can discuss certain aspects of their lives which the others in the group also share. Examples include men's and women's meetings, gay and lesbian meetings, beginner's meetings, and young people's meetings.

Keep in mind, however, that "the only requirement for AA membership is a desire to stop drinking." According to the AA traditions, no one can be kept out of a meeting because he or she does not meet some special interest criterion. For example, a woman cannot be excluded from a men's meeting and vice versa. Meetings that do not follow these traditions are not official AA group meetings.

**Some examples of special interest
AA meetings are those for men,
women, gay men, lesbians,
physicians, young people.**

"Listed" meetings are those which are included in the local list of AA meetings published by AA Intergroup or Central Office. When a meeting is not listed, it is not an official AA group meeting. Some examples of unlisted meetings include meetings for physicians, members of Congress, and celebrities. Because it can be dangerous for alcoholics to think in terms of being "special," "different," or "unique" where their alcoholism is concerned, physicians, politicians, and celebrities generally also attend regular AA group meetings.

SIZE AND LENGTH OF MEETINGS

Meetings range in size from the very small (six to eight people or fewer) to the very large (several hundred). An average-sized meeting in a large city is thirty to fifty members.

Most meetings last one hour or an hour and a half. Lunchtime meetings generally last an hour, but some people come late and leave early because of lunch hour restrictions.

**Most meetings last an hour
or an hour and a half.**

"BAD" MEETINGS

Although it is a common saying in AA that "I've never been to a bad meeting," the fact is that some meetings *are* bad. Even a good meeting can have an off night, of course, and some good AA meetings are better than others. A "bad" meeting is something different. "Bad" meetings are meetings that do not conform to AA principles and traditions, and so work against the interests of those present rather than for them. Usually, but not always, a bad meeting is one in which there are no old-timers to add stability and keep the newcomers firmly in AA principles and traditions.

One of the ways to identify a bad meeting is by the feeling you get about it. If you don't feel a sense of acceptance, love, and safety and a genuine sharing of experience, strength, and hope, there is either something wrong with you that day or with the meeting. Check yourself first. If it's not you, check the meeting.

There are some bad meetings in AA. Avoid them.

Here are some examples of bad meetings:

- Meetings characterized by psychobabble, i.e., meetings in which psychological theories and terminology are discussed rather than alcoholism, the Twelve Steps, and staying sober.
- Meetings with cross-talk, i.e., people give each other advice and offer "solutions" in response to earlier sharings. The tone of the meeting deteriorates into lecturing, preaching, and advice-giving rather than a sharing of experience, strength, and hope.
- Meetings in which AA members whine, complain, blame, and pity themselves rather than focus on appropriate actions, AA principles, and the Twelve Steps. In other words, the meetings are centered on the problem rather than on the solution.
- Meetings that focus on issues other than alcoholism and recovery, e.g., childhood, parents, inner child, or some other topic not directly related to our disease and our recovery from it.
- Meetings that exclude any alcoholic who has a desire to get sober, regardless of the reason for the exclusion except disruptive activity in the meeting.
- Meetings in which newcomers are taken advantage of sexually, emotionally, or financially.
- Meetings that are regularly dominated by "war stories" and "drunkalogues."

Whenever you run across a bad meeting, leave it in favor of one that works for you. AA is, after all, a collection of sober alcoholics who exhibit the full range of human qualities from good to evil. As the old AA saying goes, "If you sober up a horse thief, what you get is a sober horse thief." While the vast majority of AA members are earnestly working their AA program and will help you in any way they can, there are also con artists as well as selfish individuals who will ignore you or take advantage of you. Their numbers are few, but they do exist. Therefore, be aware of that possibility. We should not be cynical about AA or the world, but neither should we be naive. The good news is that the good meetings and good people in AA are in the vast majority. Stick with the winners.

AA's Meeting in Print

The *A.A. Grapevine* is AA's pocket-sized monthly journal sent to all members who subscribe. It is sometimes called "our meeting in print." The *Grapevine* contains a monthly calendar of AA events, regular features, and special articles on issues and topics of importance to AA members. It has been published since June 1944.

Chapter 17

Finding the Right Meeting for You

This chapter and the three following chapters are mainly for people who are members of groups that have traditionally been (or still are) discriminated against in our culture. You may be a gay man or lesbian, African American or Spanish-speaking, dually diagnosed (those who have an emotional or psychiatric disorder along with alcoholism), just released from prison, or any combination of the above.

These chapters have two purposes:

- To help you find the right meeting so you will be comfortable in AA from the start. AA members are sober and working on their program and their spirituality, but they are still subject to the prejudices of the world. It is possible that you might find a prejudiced first meeting and so reject all of AA on the basis of that single experience. Such a decision would be tragic, because *there is a meeting that is just right for you.*

**There is an AA meeting
that is just right for you.**

- To describe behavior that certain special populations may need to adopt in order to comply with some AA traditions. That does not mean that you will have to deny any part of you, only that AA custom supports certain behavior and discourages other behavior. By knowing the difference, you will fit into the AA Fellowship and find recovery from the very beginning.

When attending an AA meeting,
it's important to respect AA traditions.

THE ONLY REQUIREMENT FOR AA MEMBERSHIP

In accordance with AA's Third Tradition, the only requirement for membership in Alcoholics Anonymous is a desire to stop drinking. Achieving this ideal, however, depends upon the willingness of the group to override whatever prejudices, if any, it may have toward a special-population newcomer. It also depends upon the willingness of the new AA member to conform to the standards of behavior that are necessary for AA to function properly. Both parties, in other words, must keep the ideal in front of them as they try to achieve it.

AA is open to all alcoholics.

Each of us in AA may be sober, but we bring with us all the character defects of our drinking days until we can eliminate them through the AA program. The prejudices against minorities that afflict society as a whole afflict some AA groups as well. Prejudice does exist among some people within AA. It is not, however, everywhere in AA. In the earliest days of your sobriety, it may be best to check out a special interest meeting or to go to a group where you can feel confident that you will be welcomed. If you search for it, you *will* find the right group for you.

AA'S SINGLENESS OF PURPOSE

AA's Fifth Tradition states, "Each group has but one primary purpose—to carry its message to the alcoholic who still suffers." This Tradition is fundamental to Alcoholics Anonymous. AA claims specialized knowledge about only one thing: how to recover from alcoholism. In the more than sixty years since AA's founding, AA has been tempted many times to expand its purpose and program. But AA has always resisted that temptation.

AA's single purpose is to help alcoholics achieve sobriety.

Instead, AA has left it to other groups to modify the Twelve Steps to meet their special requirements. And many groups have done so. Some, such as Al-Anon, use AA's exact Twelve Steps. Others have modified them slightly for their specific addiction or disorder, such as Narcotics Anonymous, Cocaine Anonymous, Overeaters Anonymous, Emotions Anonymous, Sex and Love Addicts Anonymous, Gamblers Anonymous, and Dual Recovery Anonymous. There are thought to be more than fifteen million Americans in some form of Twelve Step recovery in dozens and dozens of different Twelve Step fellowships, all based on the AA model.[1]

There are dozens of other Twelve Step groups to help with other addictions and disorders.

Bill Wilson wrote of AA's experience, "We saw that the more A.A. minded its own business the greater its general influence would become. . . . Today we understand and accept this paradox: The more A.A. sticks to its primary purpose, the greater will be its helpful influence everywhere."[2] But there is an even better reason for AA to stick to what it knows best: survival. Many organizations have been torn apart by controversy because they ventured into fields in which they had insufficient experience or knowledge. As Bill Wilson wrote, "We think we should do one thing well rather than many things to which we are not called."[3]

The result of this single focus on alcoholism is AA's "Singleness of Purpose" statement. For a closed AA meeting, the statement reads as follows, "This is a closed meeting of Alcoholics Anonymous. In support of AA's singleness of purpose, attendance at closed meetings is limited to persons who have a desire to stop drinking. If you think you have a problem with alcohol, you are welcome to attend this meeting.

We ask that when discussing problems, we confine ourselves to those problems as they relate to alcohol."

In other words, all alcoholics are welcome in AA. As alcoholics, we can share our experience, strength, and hope with each other about our recovery from alcoholism. If we have a disorder or addiction in addition to alcoholism, however, we are asked *not* to share it in an AA meeting except as it relates to our recovery from alcoholism. AA can only help with our alcoholism.

**AA sharing is limited to
recovery from alcoholism.**

Chapter 18

Dually Addicted, or Cross-Addicted, Alcoholics

"Dually addicted," or "cross-addicted," alcoholics are addicted to alcohol and to another drug. These AA members can accommodate themselves to an AA meeting by limiting their sharing to alcoholism. It is possible to talk about our years of addiction as an alcoholic even when that addiction included other drugs. It is also possible, therefore, to translate AA in our own minds so that it applies to our other addictions without violating AA's tradition of discussing alcoholism only. In our heads, for example, "don't drink" becomes "don't drink or use."

Dually addicted AA members talk only about their alcoholism.

AA meetings that routinely discuss drug addiction in addition to alcoholism are not in compliance with AA Traditions. An AA pamphlet states, "Our A.A. group conscience, as voiced by the General Service Conference, has recommended that . . . 'alcohol and pill' meetings *not* be listed in our A.A. directories. . . . The primary purpose of any A.A. group is to carry the A.A. message to *alcoholics*. Experience with alcohol is one thing all A.A. members have in common. It is misleading to hint or give the impression that A.A. solves other problems or knows what to do about addiction to drugs."[1]

And yet, as it becomes more accepted that anyone addicted to *any* drug must remain abstinent from *all* drugs, people whose drug of choice is not necessarily alcohol typically find AA meetings relevant to their recovery needs. More AA groups are becoming tolerant of people who are not "pure" alcoholics, mainly because pure alcoholics are becoming rarer and rarer. In fact, Dr. Bob, AA's cofounder, was dually addicted. His official biography states, "Instead of taking the morning drink, which he craved, Dr. Bob turned to what he described as 'large doses of sedatives' to quiet the jitters, which distressed him terribly. He contracted what in later years would be called a pill problem, or dual addiction."[2]

Some addiction treatment counselors tell all their addicted patients to go to AA regardless of whether or not they are also alcoholics. Judges also sentence drug offenders to attend AA even if they have not been diagnosed as, or admitted to being, alcoholics. Drug addicts who are *not* also alcoholics are welcome to attend open meetings of AA, but they are generally discouraged from attending closed meetings reserved for alcoholics only. Even in open meetings, they are expected to limit their sharing to alcoholism. Therefore, drug addicts who are not alcoholics are probably better served by Narcotics Anonymous, Cocaine Anonymous, or another Twelve Step group specifically designed for their addiction.

Narcotics Anonymous (NA), for example, was formed in southern California in July 1953. NA uses the same Twelve Steps as AA except that the word "addiction" is substituted for "alcohol" in Step One, and "addicts" is substituted for "alcoholics" in Step Twelve. The basic text of NA, *Narcotics Anonymous,* explains the NA program. Thousands of NA meetings are held regularly throughout the United States.

Narcotics Anonymous (NA) is a Twelve Step group for drug addiction.

If AA seems too restricting, remember there are many other Twelve Step programs, and most of us can eventually find a place in which to discuss our other addictions or diagnoses.

Chapter 19

Dually Diagnosed Alcoholics

AA members who have an emotional or psychotic disorder in addition to alcoholism are called "dually diagnosed or dually disordered." The other diagnosis may be major depression, manic depression (bipolar disorder), personality disorder, panic disorder, and so on. As an alcoholic, you are welcome in AA regardless of any other disorder you may have. However, as with the dually addicted, dually diagnosed individuals are expected to limit their sharing in AA meetings to their alcoholism. You may discuss your other disorder with your friends in AA and with your sponsor. But you are usually not welcome to discuss it in an AA meeting except as it directly relates to your alcoholism and your desire to stay sober.

> **Dually diagnosed alcoholics are**
> **welcome in AA, but their sharing**
> **should be limited to their alcoholism.**

As with the dually addicted, numerous Twelve Step programs exist for the dually diagnosed. You may wish to attend the meetings of one of these groups. Some examples are Emotions Anonymous, Dual Disorders Anonymous, Obsessive-Compulsive Anonymous, Neurotics Anonymous, Emotional Health Anonymous, Depressed Anonymous, and Phobics Anonymous. Many alcoholics who suffer from serious depression upon entering AA find that their depression lifts and is no longer a problem after a period of sobriety. For others, this is not the case, and they need to seek help for the separate diagnosis. Bill Wilson, for example, battled serious depression in his sobriety.

Other Twelve Step programs exist
for those with a dual diagnosis.

Dually diagnosed individuals who take medications for their other disorder face special challenges in AA. Although AA is concerned with alcoholism, we know that the use of other mind-altering drugs is likely to lead us back to alcohol. For that reason, many AA members are opposed to the use of any mind-altering chemical. As a dually diagnosed individual, however, you may need to take prescribed medications in order to successfully treat another disorder.

If you tell other AA members that you use prescription drugs, you may run into a problem. The potential problem is that an uniformed AA member (and there are lots of them) may tell you to stop using the prescribed medication because it is "against AA principles." They may try to shame you into stopping or otherwise make you uncomfortable. They may even tell you that you are not really sober because you are taking the prescription drug. They may be trying to help you or they may be malicious. Either way, they are wrong. AA's official position on taking medication is very clear. It is contained in the AA pamphlet *The A.A. Member—Medications and Other Drugs.*

The pamphlet reads in part, ". . . just as it is wrong to enable or support any alcoholic to become readdicted to any drug, it's equally wrong to deprive any alcoholic of medication which can alleviate or control other disabling physical and/or emotional problems."[1] AA members are not your physicians, and they should not function as if they were. Your use of prescribed medications is between you and your physician *only*. It is nobody else's decision and nobody else's business.

AA is not against dual diagnosis members
taking their prescribed medication.

If an AA member gives you a hard time for taking prescribed medication, you may wish to make the points listed on the next page.

On the other hand, you may not. But the points are valid in case you want to talk about the issue:

1. Explain that you need your medication. You have discussed both the medication and your alcoholism with your physician. Prescribing nonaddicting medication is the accepted medical treatment for your disorder even though you are an alcoholic.
2. Remind the AA member that he or she is not your physician.
3. Explain that knowledgeable physicians don't prescribe addictive drugs for alcoholics. It is no longer even necessary with the great array of nonaddictive medications available today.
4. Remind the AA member that telling you to stop taking your prescribed medication is contrary to AA's official position. Ask the person not to bring it up again.

It may also be helpful to

1. Call your sponsor and talk about your medication if you feel shamed or pressured.
2. Find a physician who is in recovery or who is familiar with alcoholism and Twelve Step recovery so you can discuss your situation together.
3. Talk with your physician about the nature of the drug you are using and why you need to take it. By doing so, you can satisfy yourself that it is nonaddictive and that it is appropriate to take.

In the final analysis, we have to remember that AA members are not perfect and that some of them meddle in things that they don't know anything about and that are none of their business. Ignore them as best you can. Follow the guidelines in this chapter and the AA pamphlet, and you can steer a guilt-free course that will serve you well.

**It is not the business of AA members
to give other AA members advice
about whether or not to take a
prescribed medication.**

Chapter 20

Special Meetings and Groups

GAY MEN AND LESBIANS

In many cities, gay and lesbian meetings are listed in the schedule of meetings published by Intergroup. If you are a gay man or lesbian who is new to AA, you may wish to start with one of these meetings. The camaraderie and the sense of family can be very reassuring. You may also wish to read the AA pamphlet *A.A. and the Gay/Lesbian Alcoholic*. It contains stories by sober gay and lesbian alcoholics who share their experience, strength, and hope.

**A gay special interest meeting
may be a good first meeting for
gay men and lesbians.**

As with any other minority group, gay men and lesbians face more intolerance in some AA meetings than in others. People may make thoughtless comments that are insulting and destructive and aimed at no one in particular. Or they may be aimed at you. AA is like the world with all its prejudice and compassion. The key is not to be turned off by those AA members who have not yet achieved maturity, or by straight meetings that have not yet learned tolerance. There are other straight meetings where you will be welcome. And you will always be welcome in gay and lesbian meetings. Despite our limitations, our character defects, and our prejudices, we really do want each other to stay sober. We may not express that sentiment often, but we do have it. None of us wants any of us to go back to active alcoholism.

Prejudice exists in some,
but not all AA meetings.

EX-OFFENDERS

The United States and Canada have been divided into ninety-one areas, each with a Correctional Facility Committee to help AA members who are just released from prison. Six months prior to a prisoner's release, AA World Services writes to the chairperson of the Correctional Facility Committee in the area to find someone who will make a prerelease contact with the prisoner. This contact person will take the prisoner to his or her first meeting and ease the transition to the outside. If the time is shorter, World Services will send the local office a list of prisoners about to be released, and the local office arranges for a contact. In this way, alcoholics leaving prison have a specific AA member who will take them to their first meeting on the outside and help them get started.

AA members can be very accepting of ex-offenders, but that is not always the case. As with other special populations, it is important not to give up on AA if your first experience is a bad one. There are meetings where you will be welcome.

AA has a long history of working
with alcoholics in prisons.

RACIAL AND ETHNIC MINORITIES

While prejudice against African Americans, Native Americans, Latinos, and other racial and ethnic minorities is not common in AA, it still occurs. Many ethnic and racial groups have formed their own AA groups in reaction to this situation. Segregated neighborhoods and communities also contribute to the existence of segregated groups. The desire to celebrate culturally specific spiritual ideals and practices also attracts people of the same background to meetings. None of these segregation practices has AA approval. The common disease and singleness of purpose all alcoholics share usually override *all* differences in AA members—economic, racial, cultural, religious, educational, occupational, gender, *any*thing.

GENDER-SPECIFIC MEETINGS

AA permits women-only and men-only meetings as long as no one who wants to attend is excluded because of his or her sex. Some meetings do exclude the opposite sex, at least in principle, and when they do, they are not official AA meetings. Also, in a true AA meeting, gender-specific issues are discussed *only* as they relate to the members' alcoholism and sobriety. If the topics veer too far off sobriety and become focused on gender issues for their own sake, the meeting is not an AA meeting. If you choose to continue attending such a meeting, be sure that you're also attending a real AA group meeting. Remember, sobriety is our *first* priority.

THE AA INTERGROUP OR CENTRAL OFFICE IS YOUR PRIMARY CONTACT

In order to find a special interest meeting or a regular meeting that really fits, call your local Intergroup or Central Office. The local office is your primary contact, and it publishes a schedule of AA meetings in your area. AA World Services in New York can serve as a backup. The local office will know which local meetings are gay, which are Spanish-speaking, which are single sex, and whether or not there are any meetings specifically for ex-offenders in your area.

**Ask your local Intergroup
or Central Office to help
you find the right meeting.**

Chapter 21

Meeting Customs and Etiquette

Alcoholics Anonymous is a friendly and loose organization. As the Third Tradition states, "The only requirement for AA membership is a desire to stop drinking." No one is admitted to AA and no one can be expelled. We are all AA members when we say we are.

> **We are AA members when we say we are. A desire to stop drinking is the only admission requirement.**

Nevertheless, like all societies, AA has a set of customs that prescribe appropriate behavior. Customs vary significantly from one part of the country to another and sometimes from one meeting to another. There is no official AA position on most of these matters. This chapter is based on my own meeting experience. Your experience may differ.

ANNOUNCEMENTS

AA-related announcements are made at different times in meetings in different parts of the country. For example, they are made halfway through the meeting in the East (during what is called "the secretary's break"), at the beginning of the meeting in the Midwest, and at the end of the meeting in the South and West. Also during announcements, new AA members, out of town visitors, and others who are new to the meeting are asked to identify themselves. An exception is the Southwest, where visitors and newcomers identify

themselves at the beginning of the meeting even though announcements are made at the end. If the meeting uses the chip system (see
page 83), chips are also given at the break or at the end of the meeting.

> **Newcomers and visitors to an AA
> meeting are asked to identify themselves
> by their first name so they can be
> welcomed by the group.**

ARRIVING ON TIME

Except for noon meetings when some people come late or leave
early because of lunchtime schedules, it is customary to arrive at an
AA meeting on time and not to leave early. It is okay to get up for coffee (although most people do that before the meeting or at the break)
or to use the rest room.

BIRTHDAYS AND ANNIVERSARIES

AA members celebrate the anniversaries of their last drink. In the
South and West, these celebrations are called "birthdays," and in the
East and Midwest they are generally called "anniversaries." The term
"birthday" seems particularly appropriate—for those of us escaping
active alcoholism, life in recovery has been a rebirth. In some AA
groups, one meeting a month is devoted entirely to these celebrations.

> **AA members celebrate the anniversary
> of their sobriety date. In some meetings,
> it's called a birthday.**

Meetings in different parts of the country celebrate birthdays in
very different ways. At a birthday meeting in the South, for example,
each birthday celebrant speaks, "Happy Birthday" is sung, and cake
and ice cream are served. In the East, the celebration is not as elabo-
rate. In the East and West, often someone speaks for the celebrant at
the meeting.

CHIP SYSTEM

Some meetings use the "chip system" to recognize a person's length of sobriety. Medallions called "chips" are given out to mark different periods of sobriety. The first chip is called the "desire chip" or "twenty-four-hour chip" and is given to anyone who has a desire to stop drinking. It is given to newcomers and to those who have relapsed and want to trade in a "wet" one for a "dry" one.

**Chips are AA medallions given
to celebrate periods of sobriety.**

Chips may be given to celebrate one month of continuous sobriety, two months, three months, six months, one year, eighteen months, and annually thereafter. Many AA members, especially newcomers, carry their chips with them to remind themselves of their commitment to sobriety. Some members carry their desire chip while others carry their most recent birthday/anniversary chip. It is said that AA members who are about to drink should first put their chip under their tongue. If the chip melts, they can have the drink. Otherwise, they cannot.

The chip system may have had its origins in a gift from Sister Ignatia, the nurse who worked with Dr. Bob treating alcoholics at St. Thomas Hospital in Akron. "Sister Ignatia gave each of her newly released patients a Sacred Heart medallion, which she asked them to return before they took the first drink. She would occasionally give out St. Christopher medals as well. . . ."[1]

CONFIDENTIALITY

Everything that is said in an AA meeting is supposed to be confidential. It should not be repeated outside the meeting. Most AA members follow the tradition of confidentiality most of the time. But not all do. Not in every case. Therefore, while we can honestly share how we feel and what is going on with us, we should be careful about sharing anything that is *too* confidential. We need to be realistic about life rather than naive about it. AA members are like other people in the world. Some are more honest than others, and some can keep secrets better than others. Information that could truly harm us ought to be reserved for our sponsor's ears. One of the functions of a sponsor is to listen to things that are too personal for an AA meeting.

Be careful about revealing anything in an AA meeting that could hurt you if it were repeated outside the meeting.

CROSS-TALK

"Cross-talk" is when one AA member offers advice to another member during the sharing part of a meeting. AA members are expected to share their experience, strength, and hope with one another, but they are not expected to lecture or give advice. So it is against AA custom to engage in cross-talk. If an AA member asks for advice or a newcomer says something out of line, discuss the issue with him or her after the meeting.

Cross-talk is against AA customs.

DISRUPTIONS (INCLUDING DRUNK ALCOHOLICS)

Most AA meetings are civilized, and there are seldom any behavioral problems. Once in a while, a drunk alcoholic will show up and create a disturbance. Sometimes a new AA member will object to something that is said, or a disturbed person will disrupt the meeting. AA members are extraordinarily tolerant of others, but there is no reason to tolerate the disruption of a meeting. The action that needs to be taken depends upon the problem.

No one should be allowed to disrupt an AA meeting.

If someone is talking loudly, making noise, or creating a commotion, the general approach is the same for someone who is drunk as for someone who is emotionally unstable. Here are some general guidelines:

1. Don't do anything for a few minutes to see whether or not the problem will correct itself. Sometimes these individuals get quiet, and sometimes they leave the meeting.
2. If the disturbance continues, several people should quietly ask the person to step outside the meeting room for a little talk.
3. Once outside the room, tell the person that he or she is welcome in the AA meeting, but only as long as there is no disruptive behavior. As calmly and lovingly as possible, explain that you cannot allow a meeting to be disrupted. People's lives depend upon an AA meeting. All alcoholics are welcome, but only as long as they are courteous to the others present and respect their rights. Ask the person whether he or she wants to stay and be quiet or leave.
4. If the person agrees not to disrupt the meeting further, allow him or her to return. Otherwise, ask the person to leave.
5. If the disruption begins again, ask the person to leave.
6. If the person becomes violent or dangerous, call the police.
7. Do not permit threats, weapons, abusive language toward an individual, continual interrupting, or drunkenness that is disruptive in AA meetings.

If someone is speaking too long, it is the leader's call as to what to do. If the sharing runs very, very long, it is appropriate for the leader to remind the speaker that others need to speak and to ask him or her to finish quickly. If lengthy speeches are a habit of this individual, several group members may want to speak to him or her privately after the meeting.

IDENTIFYING YOURSELF

As part of sharing in a meeting, AA members traditionally identify themselves with their first names and the phrase, "I'm an alcoholic." For example, "My name is Scott, and I'm an alcoholic." This process puts everyone on a first-name basis. It also reminds us of why we are in an AA meeting. We are still alcoholics even when we are not drinking.

"My name is _____,
(Your first name)
and I'm an alcoholic."

Bill Wilson started the practice. "Never one to pass up an imaginative or appropriate idea, Bill probably picked up this custom from the early Oxford Group days. . . . At the O.G. [Oxford Group] meetings Bill and Lois attended during the middle 1930's, members sat in a circle for the 'sharing' sessions, and they would say, 'My name is so-and-so' to identify themselves.'"[2]

After we have identified ourselves, the other AA members respond in unison with a hearty "Hi" and our names, such as "Hi, Scott." This tradition is said to have started in Los Angeles. It is also said to have shaken up the Eastern AA members when they first encountered it.[3]

"Hi, _____**."**
(Your first name)

INTERRUPTING

It is considered inappropriate to interrupt anyone who is speaking. Only the meeting chairperson or leader should do so, and only in extraordinary circumstances.

It is also considered rude to whisper or talk while someone is sharing in a meeting. It seldom happens.

LAST NAMES AND TELEPHONE NUMBERS

Chapter 22, "Anonymity," explains why we use last initials instead of last names when identifying ourselves as AA members outside the Fellowship. Whether we use our last names or our last initials *within* the Fellowship is a personal decision. Either is acceptable. A 1971

General Service Conference workshop warned against increased anonymity *within* the Fellowship because it made effective communication among members more difficult.[4]

It is appropriate for us to ask for the home telephone number and last name of any AA member we meet so that we can call to get to know him or her better. Newcomers are encouraged to get the names and telephone numbers of other AA members to call when they feel lonely, scared, or in danger of relapse. This procedure is an accepted part of AA recovery. Many newcomers find it helpful to carry this list of phone numbers with them at all times. Unless we are specifically told to do so, however, we never call anyone at work. Whenever we do call another AA member, we are always careful not to say anything that would break the other person's anonymity.

> **Get the telephone numbers
> of different AA members to
> call in case you need them.**

The telephone has played an important role in AA from the very beginning. Dorothy S. M., the wife of an alcoholic who entered AA in the late 1930s, reported that "they handed out little address books with everybody's name in it. Very few people, of course, had phones then. We were all too poor. But the ones who had phone numbers, there they were."[5] Alex M., who entered AA in 1939, reported, "They'd say, 'Put a nickel in that telephone and call before you take a drink. If they don't answer, call somebody else.'"[6]

LITERATURE

Most groups have a supply of AA literature. The pamphlets are usually free and the books are inexpensive. The most commonly stocked items are the Big Book, The Twelve and Twelve, *Living Sober,* various pamphlets, and a list of local meetings (sometimes called the "Where and When"). Many of us keep a copy of the meeting schedule at home or in the car so we can go to a meeting at any time.

Be sure that newcomers get a copy of the Big Book and an AA meeting schedule.

PASSING

When we are called upon in an AA meeting, it is okay to say, "I pass" if we do not wish to share that day. However, we still identify ourselves by our first name and the expression, "I'm an alcoholic."

When called upon in an AA meeting, it is always okay to pass.

PASSING THE MEETING BASKET

AA's Seventh Tradition states, "Every A.A. group ought to be fully self-supporting, declining outside contributions." For this reason, a basket is passed during the meeting. Members traditionally put one or two dollars in the plate, but the amount of the contribution is up to the individual member. Newcomers attending their first meeting are not asked to contribute. The money collected is held by the group treasurer and used to pay rent for the meeting room, purchase coffee and cookies, buy literature, and support the local and national AA offices. In some cities in the Midwest, the basket is not actually passed, but is placed on a table.

AA accepts no money from anyone other than AA members.

OPENING THE MEETING

Most AA meetings open with a reading of the Preamble (see appendix C for the full text). In some sections of the country, the Preamble is followed by a moment of silent meditation "for the alcoholic who still suffers" and by the Serenity Prayer. Some meetings continue with a reading of "How It Works" from chapter 5 of the Big Book (see appendix C for the full text).

The format of meetings varies significantly from one part of the country to another. In the South and West, for example, each discussion meeting has a chairperson who reads the Preamble, opens and closes the meeting, and introduces the leader. In the East, each discussion meeting has a leader who opens the meeting and leads the discussion by speaking for five to twenty minutes. After his or her "lead" (or "qualifying" as it is called in the East), the meeting continues with a general discussion on the topic.

In the Midwest, the chairperson opens the meeting, but the discussion leader is chosen by those seated at each of the tables in the room. Naturally, there are exceptions to these generalizations in each area of the country. Usually, the leader calls on people he or she knows or on volunteers who have raised their hands. In smaller groups, people may talk or pass as their turns come around the circle or room. Sometimes the discussion is conducted "tag" or "California" style, although it is not necessarily the style in California. In this type of discussion, the person who is called upon shares and then calls upon the next person.

SHARING

Sharing is the process of speaking in an AA meeting. It is called "sharing" because we are expected to share our experience, strength, and hope concerning our recovery from alcoholism. We are not supposed to lecture, preach, instruct, dictate, or advise. The others present can use whatever is useful to them and ignore what is not.

VOLUNTEERING TO SHARE IN A MEETING

Most meetings rely on volunteers to share. In some meetings, it is customary to wait to be called upon. If you are about to drink or desperately need to share, volunteer regardless of the custom of the meeting. Staying sober, after all, is what meetings are about. In the East, the last five minutes of a meeting are usually reserved for those who have a "burning desire" to speak.

USING FOUR-LETTER WORDS

The use of four-letter words may be common in some AA meetings. AA members are hardly saints and the words themselves are not new to the ears of most members. Even so, the routine use of four-letter words is still offensive to many people. Courtesy suggests that they be used as infrequently as possible in sharing. Such words are better left to one-on-one conversations. AA's cofounder Dr. Bob would speak up when someone used bad language: "Dr. Bob would say, 'You have a very good lead, young man, but it would be more effective if you cleaned it up a bit.'"[7]

PART 3

ANONYMITY

Chapter 22

Anonymity

Our public relations policy is based on attraction rather than promotion; we need always maintain personal anonymity at the level of press, radio, and films.

—*Tradition Eleven of Alcoholics Anonymous (short form)*

Anonymity is the spiritual foundation of all our traditions, ever reminding us to place principles before personalities.

—*Tradition Twelve of Alcoholics Anonymous (short form)*

In my belief, the entire future of our fellowship hangs upon this vital principle [of anonymity]. . . . No A.A. principle merits more study and application than this one.[1]

—*Bill Wilson*

The principle of anonymity is so fundamental to Alcoholics Anonymous that it is part of the program's name. "Anonymity" means preserving the confidentiality of a person's comments and even presence in AA. To "break anonymity" is to reveal one's own or someone else's AA membership. The tradition of anonymity is often expressed in this simple phrase of confidentiality that is sometimes read at AA meetings:

> Who you see here,
> What you hear here,
> When you leave here,
> Let it stay here.

FOUR BASIC GUIDELINES

Four basic guidelines cover most anonymity-related situations:

1. *Never,* under any circumstances, break your own or anybody else's anonymity at the level of press, radio, television, or films.
2. *Never* break anybody else's anonymity at the personal level without permission.
3. *Never* repeat anything said at a meeting without the permission of the person who said it.
4. Break your own anonymity at a personal level outside of AA only when there is a good reason to do so.

Even with Traditions Eleven and Twelve, some confusion seems to surround anonymity within AA. This confusion is fueled by a small number of famous people who have violated the principle of anonymity at the level of press, radio, television, and films. By revealing their AA membership to the media, they have betrayed a fundamental tradition of the recovery program that has saved their lives. Their bad example trivializes the concept of anonymity and suggests that it is no longer important to contemporary recovery. Nothing could be further from the truth. It is the very bedrock on which Twelve Step recovery rests.

**Anonymity is the spiritual
foundation of all our traditions.**

A HISTORICAL PERSPECTIVE OF ANONYMITY

In the earliest days of Alcoholics Anonymous, it was proposed that celebrities who had found recovery in AA break their anonymity. The goal was to tell the world about AA's success and to spread the recovery message quicker. The founders of AA, having had no previous experience with breaking anonymity, agreed to this idea. The results were dramatic: the collapse of public anonymity so threatened the effectiveness of AA that the principle of anonymity at the media level was reinstated. Ultimately, it became the Eleventh Tradition.

**The tradition of anonymity
at the media level developed
on the basis of hard experience.**

What went wrong? It turned out to be impossible to control *who* would break anonymity and *what* would be said. Celebrities with clear heads spoke out publicly, but so did celebrities with fuzzy heads. Besides celebrities, "other [AA] members decided to break their anonymity in the media—some motivated by good will, others by personal gain. Some members devised schemes to tie in their AA affiliation with all sorts of business enterprises—insurance sales, drying-out farms, even a temperance magazine, to name a few. . . . if one person was made an exception, other exceptions would inevitably follow. To assure the unity, effectiveness, and welfare of A.A., anonymity had to be universal."[2]

ANONYMITY SERVES MANY PURPOSES

Over the years, anonymity in AA has come to represent a whole set of principles based on humility and on respect for self and others. The tradition of anonymity is much broader and much more important than many people in AA realize.

**Anonymity represents a whole set
of principles based on humility and
on respect for self and others.**

Here are some of the functions of anonymity:

Anonymity at the Personal Level

1. "At the personal level, anonymity provides protection for all members from identification as alcoholics, a safeguard often of special importance to newcomers."[3]

2. AA members have a right to the privacy of their lives. We have a right to confront our problems and work them out in the company of supportive friends. The tradition of anonymity makes growth and trust possible because it creates a safe environment in which we can risk intimacy. We can share who we are and what we feel. Anonymity makes it possible for us to talk honestly about our alcoholic lives.

Anonymity creates a safe environment in which to share and grow.

3. From a practical standpoint, the tradition of anonymity means that we don't know much about the other AA member who is sharing his or her experience, strength, and hope. As a result, we listen to the words of the person without the prejudices of cultural, personal, or socioeconomic factors. The person's bank balance, street address, alma mater, job description, and family name are unknown and unimportant.

4. Anonymity keeps us focused on principles rather than personalities. There are no "stars" in AA. There are a few gurus with clay feet, but even their "guru-ness" is based on what they say in meetings and on their contribution to the Fellowship. By focusing on the Steps and the practice of AA principles "in all our affairs" rather than on individual personalities, we grow within—and are protected by—the truths of the Fellowship.

5. Anonymity nurtures humility. It fosters equality among members.

Anonymity helps us place principles before personalities.

6. The principle of anonymity helps us focus on our similarities to others rather than on our differences. We find commonalty

and community rather than diversity and division in our individual problems and in our mutual successes. We learn to contribute to others and to the group.

7. Finally, the tradition of anonymity "reminds us that it is the A.A. message, not the messenger, that counts."[4]

**It's the AA message,
not the messenger,
that counts.**

Anonymity at the Level of Press, Radio, Television, and Films

1. "At the level of press, radio, TV, and films, anonymity stresses the equality in the Fellowship of all members by putting the brake on those who might otherwise exploit their A.A. affiliation to achieve recognition, power, or personal gain."[5]

**Anonymity both protects
AA members and stresses
their equality.**

2. Anonymity at the media level prevents a single AA member from speaking for all of AA when he or she expresses an opinion in public. Such a person may be new to AA and not knowledgeable enough about its principles to get the facts right, or he or she may have views that are inconsistent with those of AA as a whole.

3. The long-form version of AA's Tenth Tradition states, "No A.A. group or member should ever, in such a way as to implicate A.A., express any opinion on outside controversial issues—particularly those of politics, alcohol reform, or sectarian religion. The Alcoholics Anonymous groups oppose no one. Concerning such matters they can express no views whatsoever."

Anonymity keeps AA
out of controversies.

When AA members break anonymity and discuss issues such as politics or alcohol reform at the media level, they may give the impression that their views are held by Alcoholics Anonymous itself. The celebrity's comments thus have the potential of distorting the public's perception of AA.

4. Celebrities may fail to work the AA program and return to drinking after publicly announcing their AA membership. This may discourage others from joining AA by giving the impression that AA doesn't work.
5. Anonymity serves to keep runaway egos in check. Bill Wilson turned down an honorary degree from Yale University because in accepting the degree, he would have had to break his anonymity. He also turned down a cover story in *Time* magazine. Even the cofounder of AA was not above its principles.[6]

Anonymity helps us combat
alcoholic grandiosity.

6. The tradition of anonymity reminds us that we have a right to speak for ourselves, but not for other AA members.
7. The anonymity principle is also a reminder that our real responsibility to our fellow humans is in what we *do*, not just in what we say. It is in our deeds as well as in our words. Anonymity helps us resist the temptation to speak loudly of our new lives and sends us instead on a journey to create them.

Bill Wilson summarized it best when he wrote of anonymity: "It isn't just something to save us from alcoholic shame and stigma; its deeper purpose is actually to keep those fool egos of ours from running hog wild after money and public fame at A.A.'s expense. It really means personal and group sacrifice for the benefit of all A.A."[7]

**It is easy to rationalize breaking
anonymity even when it is against
AA principles to do so.**

PRESERVING ANONYMITY WHILE TALKING
ABOUT OUR ALCOHOLISM

It is not a break of anonymity to reveal to someone at the personal
or the media level that we are alcoholic. Anonymity applies *only* to AA
membership, not to the disease of alcoholism. We can, if we wish, take
out a full-page ad in the *New York Times* or go on the *CBS Evening
News* to announce our alcoholism as long as we do *not* reveal our AA
membership.

**It is *not* a violation of anonymity
to reveal our alcoholism at the
media level as long as we do *not*
reveal our AA membership.**

This distinction is very important because there are times when it
is necessary to speak out for the rights of alcoholics in recovery and for
the need for more money to further alcoholism research. If no one
spoke out against the stigma and discrimination associated with the
disease, progress would not be made.

WHEN TO BREAK ANONYMITY AT THE PERSONAL LEVEL

Dr. Bob is credited with saying, "The A.A. who hides his identity
from his fellow A.A. by using only a given name violates the
[Eleventh] Tradition just as much as the A.A. who permits his name
to appear in the press in connection with matters pertaining to A.A."[8]
In Dr. Bob's view, it was a break of the anonymity tradition to be "so
anonymous that you can't be reached by other drunks."[9]

**It is okay to use our
last names within AA.**

Breaking anonymity at the personal level outside of AA, however, is another matter. It should not be broken lightly because, once lost, it can never be regained. Newcomers are advised to wait until their feet are firmly on the ground before breaking their anonymity to anyone except family members. Because a great deal of stigma is still associated with alcoholism, we are particularly careful about breaking our anonymity at work. Job discrimination against alcoholics is common in some fields.

Be careful about breaking
anonymity at the office.

The general guideline is to break anonymity only when we have a good reason to do so. Here are some good reasons to do so:

1. *When it will help someone else.* If friends or acquaintances are in trouble with alcohol, and we can "carry the message" to them by breaking our anonymity, we should consider doing so. AA surveys show that a large proportion of AA members joined because some other AA member carried the message. Our responsibility to help others is clear. "When anyone, anywhere reaches out for help, I want the hand of A.A. always to be there. And for that: I am responsible."[10]

We break our anonymity at the
personal level when it will help
someone else for us to do so.

2. *When people in our lives have a "need to know."* Close friends, family members, and significant others may wonder about our changed lives, our "disappearance" to attend AA meetings, our new friends, or our need to call our sponsor. We break anonymity with these people on a "need to know" basis. When in doubt, we meditate on it and follow our intuition.

3. *When we think it will help us stay sober.* Admitting to someone that we are alcoholic is not an anonymity break as long as we don't reveal our AA membership. Some individuals are quite open about their alcoholism. When we think that admitting our alcoholism will help us stay sober, we do so. By the same token, if we think adding that we are an AA member (but not at the media level) will be helpful, we do that as well.

When in doubt about breaking anonymity, check with your sponsor, ask your Higher Power, and follow your intuition. If you have a nagging feeling that you shouldn't do it, don't.

POSTHUMOUS ANONYMITY

The Traditions do not suggest that we need to maintain someone's anonymity after death. Bill Wilson's page one obituary in the *New York Times* carried his full name and picture.[11] Delegates at the April 1971 General Service Conference were told that a member's anonymity after death needs to be observed "only if that was the member's expressed wish and his family's continuing desire."[12]

> **Anonymity at the media level can**
> **be broken after death unless the**
> **AA member had specified otherwise.**

PART 4

THE SURVIVAL GUIDE

Chapter 23

Common Questions About Alcohol and AA

The following questions are often asked by newcomers. The answers are strictly my own opinion. Not every AA member would agree with them.

What is the definition of "alcoholism"?

A definition of "alcoholism" that is accepted by all authorities has yet to be developed. Perhaps the best definition was proposed in 1990 by the National Council on Alcoholism and Drug Dependence (NCADD) and the American Society of Addiction Medicine (ASAM). It is a complicated definition, but alcoholism itself is a complex disease.

"Alcoholism," according to the two organizations, "is a primary, chronic disease with genetic, psychosocial, and environmental factors influencing its development and manifestations. The disease is often progressive and fatal. It is characterized by continuous or periodic: impaired control over drinking, preoccupation with the drug alcohol, use of alcohol despite adverse consequences, and distortions in thinking, most notably denial."[1]

Alcoholism is a disease with a genetic predisposition.

The American Medical Association also describes alcoholism as "a complex disease with biological, psychological and sociological components."[2] The first American to define alcoholism as a disease was Dr. Benjamin Rush. His 1874 work *An Inquiry into the Effects of Ardent Spirits on the Human Mind and Body* prescribed abstinence as the only cure.[3]

Why am I an alcoholic?

No one knows exactly what causes alcoholism (see the previous question). When I was new to AA, I spent a lot of time worrying about why I was an alcoholic. I now realize that I was trying to figure out *why* I was an alcoholic so I could find a way to drink normally again. When I finally accepted that I could not change my alcoholism, I stopped looking for the answer to the question.

**Once an alcoholic,
always an alcoholic.**

What about controlled drinking?

There is no such thing as controlled drinking for an alcoholic. The basic characteristic of alcoholism is an inability to control alcohol usage. No research study with proper methodology has ever shown that an alcoholic can return to controlled drinking. Over the years, several studies have claimed to show that alcoholics could learn to control their drinking. One such study by the Rand Corporation received widespread publicity. It has been discredited along with other studies with similar findings.[4] No form of treatment has ever permitted an alcoholic to return to normal drinking. Numerous amateurs masquerading as experts have come forth with "cures" for alcoholism or with systems for teaching alcoholics to drink normally again. They don't work. Competent medical experts are unanimous on this issue: the only treatment for alcoholism is abstinence. Period.

**Controlled drinking is not
possible for an alcoholic.**

Should I take Antabuse or NaltrExone?

"Antabuse" is the trade name for a medication called "disulfiram." Antabuse causes a person to become violently ill if he or she drinks alcohol, so it is impossible to drink alcohol while taking Antabuse. Some AA members take Antabuse because it helps them stay sober. Whether or not you choose to take Antabuse is between you and your physician. It is nobody else's business.

For some people, Antabuse is an important part of their sobriety.

Another drug, NaltrExone hydrochloride, has become available more recently. Some clinical tests have shown that NaltrExone can help alcoholism treatment by reducing craving, drinking days, and relapse rates in many alcoholics when taken as part of a treatment program that includes AA attendance.[5] As with Antabuse, whether you want to try this medication is between you and your physician.

Do I have to give up my old drinking (or using) friends?

This question is not one that has to be answered immediately. It can be taken "one day at a time." For the present, it is better not to visit with old drinking or using friends in an environment where the temptation to return to drinking or other drug use is strong. It is important to avoid slippery places in the early days of sobriety. As time goes by, you may find that your old drinking or using friends seem less interesting and their lifestyle less attractive. For the moment, though, concentrate on staying sober. If you want to visit with them, consider doing so over the telephone or in a safe environment away from alcohol.

An old drinking friend and a slippery place are a dangerous combination.

How long do I have to go to meetings?

Technically, we have to go to meetings "Just for today." In AA, we take recovery one day at a time. But many of us continue to attend meetings for the rest of our lives. In that way, we are like the victims of other chronic diseases who often have to maintain their therapeutic programs for life. While it may be possible for some to stay sober without attending meetings, the odds of remaining in recovery are better for those who attend meetings regularly. For many of us, it is not worth the risk to stop going to meetings.

**AA meetings are part of a treatment
program for an incurable disease.**

In the last year of his life, Dr. Bob continued to attend his regular King School meeting in Akron even though he was dying of cancer. Someone asked him why he continued to attend meetings instead of resting. He answered, "The first reason is that this way is working so well. Why should I take a chance on any other way? The second reason is that I don't want to deprive myself of the privilege of meeting, greeting, and visiting with fellow alcoholics. It is a pleasure to me. And the third reason is the most important. I belong at that meeting for the sake of the new man or woman who might walk through that door. I am living proof that A.A. will work as long as I work A.A., and I owe it to the new person to be there."[6]

Should I keep alcohol in the house?

Some AA members do keep alcohol at home, but others do not. It depends on how comfortable you are with having alcohol around. Some people remove the alcohol at first and then bring it back later for friends who drink. Others never serve alcohol again in their homes. It's a matter of personal preference. When in doubt, take the safer route.

**Whether or not to keep
alcohol in the house is a matter
of personal preference.**

Is it okay to joke about having a drink?

Many of us don't recommend joking around about drinking. AA members have a lot of fun, and there's a great deal of joking, but not about having a drink. There is something risky about saying, "I'll have a scotch and water" and then adding, "I'm only joking." It's too close to old habits and maybe a fantasy or two.

We don't have to deny the good times we had while drinking, but we do need to keep them in perspective by remembering what the bad times cost us. For drinking alcoholics, the "good times" don't come without bad times. Our tendency to forget the bad times and remember the good is part of denial.

Can I drink nonalcoholic beer?

In my opinion it is not a good idea to drink nonalcoholic beer, but others would disagree. I do know people with years of sobriety who do. Even so, I've never understood why. They claim they like the taste (and they probably do), but for me it's like playing with fire. As a friend of mine said to an alcoholic/cocaine addict in recovery, "You don't snort baking soda, why would you drink nonalcoholic beer?"

Most of us have a lot of alcoholic associations that come with the taste of beer. Why reactivate them? As with any decision, the basic question is this: What is the potential for good (the rewards) versus the potential for bad (the risks)? Where nonalcoholic beer is concerned, the answer for me is clear: the rewards aren't worth the risk.

**Nonalcoholic beer may
contain some alcohol and can
remind us of our drinking days.
Why take a chance?**

Is it okay to take wine with Communion?

Some AA members do drink wine in church services and some don't. Personally, I don't take the wine. I follow this policy for a simple reason. I want to be certain that I have never intentionally drunk alcohol since getting sober. The argument that I never want to raise with myself is this: How much alcohol can I safely drink? I know how my mind works. My first question to myself would be, "How tiny does the sip of wine at Communion have to be not to count? If I can have a tiny sip, can I have a little sip (which is two tiny sips)? If I can have a little sip, why not a medium sip? If a medium sip, why not half a teaspoon? If half a teaspoon, how about a whole teaspoon? If a whole teaspoon, how about two teaspoons? You can see where that kind of thinking leads me. Besides, I don't want to taste the wine. It has too many memories.

**Some AA members take
wine with Communion,
others do not.**

What about a little cough syrup that contains alcohol?

It's very risky to take cough syrup that contains alcohol. There is no difference between the standard dosage of three teaspoons of 20 proof cough syrup and one teaspoon of creme de menthe at 60 proof. The delivery system doesn't matter—alcohol is still alcohol no matter how it's distilled—and neither does the excuse. Our reason for taking alcohol has no effect on our body's reaction to it. We don't get "credit" for medicinal uses.

All alcohol can reactivate the obsession, no matter what form it is in. Alcohol-based cough syrups or alcohol-based antidiarrheals are potentially slippery. Mouthwash with alcohol is equally risky. Why take a chance? Would you gargle poison on the bet that you wouldn't swallow it? For the alcoholic, to drink or not to drink is not a social question. It is, literally, a matter of life and death. We never know what the next drunk will bring or what it will cost us.

**Avoid taking cough syrup
that contains alcohol.**

What if I take a swallow of an alcoholic drink by mistake?

Someday in sobriety you will likely, by mistake, take a swallow of alcohol from somebody else's drink. Or you will unintentionally eat ice cream with liqueur on top or something like that. It has happened to me several times. Here's what sponsors often recommend to sponsees who swallow alcohol by mistake in sobriety:

1. Spit out as much of it as you can. I pretend to choke. It doesn't matter what it looks like as long as you don't swallow any more than you already have.
2. Ask your Higher Power to protect you from relapse.
3. Call your sponsor or someone else you know in AA and explain what happened.
4. Go to a meeting as soon as you can and share the experience.
5. Forget about it and go on. You had no intention of doing it, and accidents happen. You'll be okay. (If anyone tells you to change your sobriety date, ignore them.)

If you drink alcohol by accident, spit out as much of it as you can, call your sponsor, and go to a meeting.

What if the dessert I've just been served has liqueur in it?

Don't eat it. Tell your host or hostess that you're on a diet or use some other excuse. AA members who say, "I never got drunk on bananas foster" get a laugh, but they miss the point. It is the *first* drink we take that gets us drunk, not the last. It is the first drink that sets up the compulsion that leads to the last drink. Therefore, bananas foster with alcohol left in it could get us drunk just like a glass of red wine, because it is the alcohol that sets up the compulsion to drink. *Flaming desserts do not burn off all the alcohol!* Be careful not to rationalize yourself into a slip.

Flaming desserts have some alcohol left in them.

What does it mean if I have a drinking dream?

A drinking dream could be a warning. Or it could be wish fulfillment. Or it could be a helpful reminder of how much your sobriety means to you. Or it could be something else. Tell your sponsor about it and share the dream in your next AA meeting.

**Almost everyone has a drinking
dream at one time or another.**

What if I meet an AA member on the street?

When you run into an AA member you know outside of an AA meeting, always protect that person's anonymity. We have no right to break another person's anonymity under any set of circumstances, even accidentally. If either of you is with someone else, don't say anything that would reveal that the other is an AA member. If you need to introduce the AA member but you don't know his or her last name, just give first-name introductions.

**Be careful not to break other
AA members' anonymity when
you see them outside AA.**

If you are asked how you know the other person, say from a party or business meeting, or whatever term for a social gathering you feel comfortable using.

What should I do when I'm traveling and I'm new to AA?

The following suggestions may be helpful when you're traveling:

1. Take the telephone numbers of your sponsor and of several other AA friends with you. It's safer to have several phone numbers in case someone isn't home when you call. In an emergency, call the local Intergroup/Central Office, listed in

the white pages under "Alcoholics Anonymous." If it is closed, call the AA office in New York, Chicago, or Los Angeles because it may be open.

2. Pack the Big Book, your favorite meditation book, and any other recovery or spiritual literature you regularly read.

Visiting AA meetings in exotic places can be a fun part of traveling.

3. Carry your desire chip or your birthday/anniversary chip.
4. Call the local AA Intergroup/Central Office upon your arrival to find a nearby meeting in case you need it.
5. When planning a trip abroad, call your local AA Intergroup/Central Office (or AA World Services in New York City) for the international directory of meetings. Make a list of the meetings in the cities you'll be visiting.
6. Don't get too Hungry, Angry, Lonely, or Tired while traveling.
7. Attend an AA meeting if you can.

Why has my sponsor suggested that I not make any major life changes in the first year of sobriety?

It is suggested that people new to recovery avoid making major changes in their lives during the first year of sobriety. Some examples of major changes are getting divorced, getting married, changing jobs, relocating to another city, buying a house. So many changes take place in early sobriety that it's better not to take on even more.

Also, we are not the same people at the end of our first year of recovery as we were at the start. The attitudes and outlook that we brought into recovery were not very good for making decisions. As a result, most of us would have made big mistakes had we made major decisions during our first year of sobriety. By the end of the year, we had changed mentally, emotionally, and spiritually and so had the list of things we wanted.

Try to avoid making major changes during the first year of sobriety.

However, not everyone can postpone major life decisions until the end of the first year of sobriety. When such decisions can't be postponed, we make them to the best of our ability. Nevertheless, when postponement is possible, it is usually preferable. AA provides guidelines for living, not infallible rules.

Why shouldn't I become romantically involved with anyone during the first year of sobriety?

It is suggested that people new to recovery avoid romantic or sexual relationships during their first year of sobriety. The emotional vulnerability we all experience during the first months of recovery can draw us into hasty affairs. These affairs can lead us back to drinking. Those with long-term sobriety have seen such relapses over and over. Whether from giddy infatuation or desperate disappointment, many of us have drunk over love affairs that we were incapable of handling.

We have a lot to work on during our first year, and a romantic relationship can be a major distraction from the serious business of learning to live in sobriety. We have our hands full dealing with ourselves and sorting out our lives. We are not even sure who we are, so we are hardly in a position to offer ourselves to others in intimate relationships.

Romantic relationships are best avoided in the first year.

In early recovery, it is easy to transfer our dependence on chemicals to our romantic attachment. We may expect our romantic partner to meet all our emotional needs and to solve all our emotional problems. When these expectations are not met, we may become angry, bitter, and inclined to drink. Or we try to substitute a romantic relationship for working the Twelve Steps, and so risk our recovery or make little or no headway in it. Substituting a romantic obsession for the AA program is an "easier, softer way" that doesn't work.

What is the "Thirteenth Step"?

There is no thirteenth step in AA. The term is used to describe sexual advances made by one member of the Fellowship toward newcomers or other AA members who should not be approached in that manner (such as sponsors toward sponsees).

Human beings are human beings whether sober or not, and sexual desire is part of that humanity. Whether or not we act on that desire, however, is up to us. It is a matter of choice. It is irresponsible and inappropriate to make sexual advances toward (1) AA members who have less than a year's sobriety and (2) sponsees. Because new members are emotionally vulnerable, easily manipulated in AA's environment of trust and intimacy, and highly subject to relapse when involved in sexual intimacy, thirteenth stepping them is unacceptable. Newcomers need to be aware that thirteenth stepping does go on, and they need to protect themselves as best they can.

**Be careful about
thirteenth steppers.**

What does the Alcoholics Anonymous symbol mean?

The AA symbol is a circle enclosing a triangle. The circle stands for the whole world of AA and the triangle stands for AA's Three Legacies of Recovery, Unity, and Service.

Bill Wilson wrote, "The priests and seers of antiquity regarded the circle enclosing the triangle as a means of warding off spirits of evil, and A.A.'s circle and triangle of Recovery, Unity, and Service has certainly meant all of that to us and much more."[7] The symbol was unveiled at AA's twentieth anniversary conference in St. Louis in 1955.[8]

**The AA symbol was
adopted in 1955.**

How did Alcoholics Anonymous get its name?

It is generally agreed that AA took its name from the title of the Big Book.[9] After the New York AA groups separated from the Oxford Group in 1937, they referred to themselves as a "nameless bunch of alcoholics." "From this phrase," wrote Bill Wilson, "it was only a step to the idea of 'Alcoholics Anonymous.'"[10] *Alcoholics Anonymous,* as a book title, was being discussed as early as October 1938. According to Lois Wilson, Bill's wife, a former writer for the *New Yorker* magazine in New York AA dreamed up the book's title.[11] In 1939, Clarence S. named the AA group he was forming in Cleveland after the Big Book, calling it Alcoholics Anonymous. This was the first clear usage of the name for an AA group.[12]

**The title *Alcoholics Anonymous*
was dreamed up by a writer
for *The New Yorker.***

What is a "dry drunk"?

We are on a "dry drunk" when we engage in alcoholic thinking and behavior even though we have not returned to drinking. Dry drunks result from a renewal of alcoholic grandiosity and are characterized by[13]

- Increasing resentments.
- Taking back the surrender we made in the First Step: denying the powerlessness over alcohol and the unmanageability of our lives.
- Forgetting the bottom that brought us into AA.
- Reasserting our own wills rather than turning them over to our Higher Power.

- Developing a sense of being "unique," "an exception," or "different from other alcoholics."

In a dry drunk, life becomes almost too painful to bear in a sober state, and the threat of relapse is high.[14] A dry drunk is a warning that we may slip. Bill Wilson wrote, "These emotional 'dry benders' often led straight to the bottle."[15] One of the best ways out of a dry drunk is to work with another still-suffering alcoholic.

What is "stinking thinking"?

The phrase "stinking thinking" refers to old thought patterns and perceptions that can lead us back to drinking. Some examples of stinking thinking are blaming others, fault-finding, alcoholic grandiosity, skipping meetings, self-centeredness, and taking other people's inventory while refusing to look at our own character defects. Stinking thinking is a warning sign that we are not working our AA program. We get out of stinking thinking by working the Steps, calling our sponsor, sharing at a meeting, reading the Big Book, praying or meditating, working with another alcoholic, changing our attitudes, doing a mini-inventory, or making a gratitude list.

What is the difference between a "recovering" and a "recovered" alcoholic?

Some members of Alcoholics Anonymous call themselves "recovering" alcoholics whereas other members call themselves "recovered" alcoholics. Those who use the term "recovering" do so because recovery is an ongoing process that is never complete. There is no cure for alcoholism. Since sobriety is a one-day-at-a-time process, these AA members don't feel secure in saying they are "recovered."

Those who use the term "recovered" do so because they see themselves as having recovered from alcoholism for the one day in which they find themselves. This term follows the medical guideline that says someone has recovered from a disease after a certain period of time has passed. A cancer patient, for example, is said to have recovered if the cancer has not recurred within five years. The term "recovered" also reminds the public that alcoholism is a disease from which recovery *is* possible. No one's recovery from alcoholism (or cancer) is certain. But those who have established a reasonable period of sobriety in AA have, statistically, a good chance of remaining sober for the rest of their lives, one day at a time.

AA literature uses the term "recovered." The foreword to the first edition of the Big Book opens with this sentence: "We, of Alcoholics Anonymous, are more than one hundred men and women who have recovered from a seemingly hopeless state of mind and body. To show other alcoholics *precisely how we have recovered* is the main purpose of this book."[16] The term also appears in chapter 9 of the Big Book, "We have recovered, and have been given the power to help others."[17]

Some AA members have resolved the issue by referring to themselves as "recovering" in AA meetings and as "recovered" when they talk publicly about their alcoholism (but not about their AA membership!).

Chapter 24

Seventy-Five Ways to Stay Sober

This chapter lists seventy-five ways to stay sober. There are many more, of course. The most important action we take is to work the Twelve Steps. Meetings, sponsors, service work, and our relationship with our Higher Power are also important. All these aspects of the program help us stay sober.

To avoid taking that first drink, we

AA meetings . . .

 1. Arrive early and stay late to talk with other Fellowship members.
 2. Choose a home group and attend often enough to know the people well.
 3. Share in the meeting how we are doing and what we are feeling.
 4. Introduce ourselves to one person we don't already know.
 5. Ask someone for his or her telephone number.
 6. Give our telephone number to a newcomer.
 7. When we're new, do ninety meetings in ninety days.

8. Attend AA meetings regularly.

Working the Steps . . .

 9. Take the First Step daily.
 10. Read and study the Big Book and the Twelve and Twelve.
 11. Work the Steps in order, trying to understand each Step and then applying its principles to our lives.
 12. Practice AA principles in all our affairs.

13. Work the Steps daily.

Spirituality . . .

14. In the morning, ask our Higher Power to keep us sober and thank Him at night for doing so.
15. Ask God to help us get rid of the resentments that are eating us up.
16. Pray for willingness.
17. Pray to be relieved of the bondage of self.
18. Do a morning meditation.
19. Work on developing humility.
20. Practice honesty.
21. Ask God to reveal His will for us and to give us the strength and courage to carry it out.
22. Forgive others and ourselves.
23. Do one good deed a day for which we take no credit.

24. Maintain a conscious contact with our Higher Power.

Sponsors . . .

25. Get a sponsor and stay in regular contact.
26. Ask our sponsors to help us work the Steps.
27. Sponsor somebody.

28. Call our sponsors regularly.

Reaching out and helping others . . .

29. Talk with at least one AA member every day.
30. Share our experience, strength, and hope with others.
31. Ask for help when we need it.
32. Make a Twelfth Step call.

33. Carry a list of AA telephone numbers with us at all times and use them when we need to.

34. Don't isolate.

35. Take a meeting to the local corrections facility.
36. Help clean up at a meeting—replacing chairs, removing ashtrays, and so on.
37. Say "yes" when asked to lead, chair, speak, or otherwise be of service unless we have a very good reason to say "no."
38. Answer telephones for Intergroup.

39. Volunteer for service work.

Reading . . .

40. Read AA pamphlets and other literature about the Fellowship.
41. Subscribe to the *A.A. Grapevine,* AA's monthly journal or "our meeting in print."

42. Read something inspiring every day.

Act on the following slogans . . .

43. Don't drink.
44. Take life and sobriety one day at a time.
45. Keep it simple.
46. Let go and let God.
47. Live and let live.
48. Don't get too Hungry, Angry, Lonely, or Tired (H.A.L.T.).
49. Avoid slippery places.
50. Put first things first.
51. Stick with the winners.
52. Do the next right thing.

53. Place principles before personalities.
54. Easy does it, but do it.
55. Go with the flow.
56. Accept life on life's terms.
57. Remember that it's progress not perfection.
58. Turn it over.
59. Keep coming back.
60. Preserve our anonymity at the level of press, radio, television, and films.

61. Maintain an attitude of gratitude.

In an emergency, we . . .

62. Ask our Higher Power to keep us sober.
63. Say the Serenity Prayer.
64. Think the drink through.
65. Remember our last drunk.
66. Immediately leave wherever we are before we take the drink.
67. Take it one minute at a time if necessary.
68. Remember that we are willing to go to any lengths to stay sober.
69. Call our sponsor or anybody we know in AA.
70. Go to a meeting.
71. Make a mental or written gratitude list.
72. Put our twenty-four-hour chip or birthday/anniversary chip in our mouth. If it dissolves, we can have the drink.
73. Repeat the first three Steps.
74. Remember that this, too, whatever it is, shall pass.
75. *No matter what happens, don't take the drink.*

**In an emergency, do whatever
is necessary to stay sober.**

Chapter 25

You Can Have a Good Time Sober

Part of getting started in AA is recognizing that alcohol still exists in the world even though it is no longer part of our personal lives. Alcohol will always be available to us, but working our program and going to AA gives us the ability to turn it down. One day at a time, we choose not to drink. Yet many times, we will find ourselves in situations where alcohol is being served. Sometimes alcohol is encountered at a gathering of people from work or at a business lunch, sometimes at a party, sometimes at a special occasion like a wedding.

Over the years, AA members have developed specific guidelines and techniques to use when attending parties or functions where alcohol is served. This AA wisdom is particularly helpful when we are new to the Fellowship. Sobriety is about being alive, after all, and part of life is partying and socializing. Sometimes that partying will involve the use of alcohol by others. There is no reason not to party in sobriety. But we need to honestly look at our motives, plan well, and use a few techniques that have proven useful.

**There is no reason
not to party in recovery.**

SIX BASIC QUESTIONS

Before attending any party or function where alcohol will be served, ask yourself the following six questions. They will help you determine your motives for going and your state of mind. When we're new to sobriety, we have to be careful about visiting such places. It is difficult to do safely in early sobriety what we can do with ease later on.

1. *Do I have a legitimate reason for going where alcohol will be served?*

The Big Book states, "So our rule is not to avoid a place where there is drinking, *if we have a legitimate reason for being there.* That includes bars, nightclubs, dances, receptions, weddings.... Therefore, ask yourself on each occasion, 'Have I any good social, business, or personal reason for going to this place?' ... If you answer these questions satisfactorily, you need have no [fear about going] ... But be sure you are on solid spiritual ground before you start and that your motive in going is thoroughly good."[1]

We don't have to avoid a place where there is drinking, if we have a legitimate reason for being there.

2. *What is the state of my spiritual condition?*

The Big Book reminds us that "We are not cured of alcoholism. What we really have is a daily reprieve contingent on the maintenance of our spiritual condition."[2] Therefore, we check our spiritual condition before going to a slippery place *even if we have a legitimate reason for being there.* We avoid such places when our conscious contact with our Higher Power is weak. We also check the state of our self-centeredness, our willfulness, and our grandiosity. If we are in a period of self-will run riot, we avoid places that might tempt us to drink.

Check your spiritual condition before going to a potentially slippery place.

3. *What is the state of my mental and physical condition?*

We check our mental and physical condition before going to a place that might prove to be slippery. Are we hungry, angry, lonely, or tired? Are we depressed or resentful? Are we full of self-pity—"on the pity pot"? If we are, then we stay away. These conditions weaken our defenses and make us more likely to drink.

4. Do I have a party plan?

A party plan prepares our thinking so we don't fall into old thought patterns if something unexpected happens and old behaviors and habits try to reassert themselves. In other words, we don't wander naively into a dangerous situation. Instead, we develop a plan that may include the following elements:

- We take our list of AA telephone numbers with us to use in case we feel like drinking and need to talk with someone.
- We think through what we will order to drink before we get there.
- We anticipate what we will say to old friends who may not be aware that we are no longer drinking or using other drugs.
- We ask our Higher Power for guidance and support.
- We determine to leave immediately if our sobriety is in danger.

> **Having a "party plan" means having thought through the party situation in advance.**

The longer we are in AA, the easier and more natural it feels to refuse an alcoholic beverage. Nonrecovering alcoholics and alcohol and other drug abusers will often pressure us to drink or use other drugs, so we have to be firm with them. If they won't take "no" for an answer, we ask them this question, "Why is it so threatening to you that I'm not drinking (or using)?" If that doesn't work, we might say something like, "Maybe you need to look at your own drinking (or drug use) if you're so uncomfortable with me not joining you." We may never get invited back, but at least they won't ask us again if we want a drink!

**The people who will pressure us
to drink are usually those with a
drinking problem themselves.**

Remember that one-third of Americans *do not drink at all, ever, under any set of circumstances.* Of the other two-thirds who do drink, some percentage are not drinking at a given party for any number of reasons. And the great majority of people don't use illegal drugs. *There is nothing odd about not drinking.* Many of us have proven this fact to ourselves by watching how many people at parties order a "Perrier and lime" or a club soda or a Coke.

**One-third of Americans
don't drink at all.**

When we go to a party where drinking will occur, it helps to bring a friend in recovery. There is added safety in having someone along who knows we don't drink and with whom we can share our feelings. Our friend in recovery will provide a gentle but persuasive reminder of the benefits we have received from sobriety if the false promises of alcohol present themselves. Furthermore, we will feel less lonely and less pressured to turn to alcohol for relief.

**When attending a party where
drinking will occur, it helps to
bring a friend in recovery.**

Some recovering people who attend a party without a friend in recovery will tell the host confidentially that they have given up alcohol. They do it in order to reduce the pressure to drink and so that at least one other person will know they can't drink.

5. Do I have an "escape plan"?

An "escape plan" is a way to leave a party, meeting, or gathering where alcohol is being served. This way out may mean taking our own car rather than riding with someone else. It may mean going with someone in recovery who understands our situation and could drive us home if we needed to leave. Or it may mean carrying enough money to pay for a bus or taxicab ride home.

**Always have a way to leave a situation
where alcohol will be served.**

If our sobriety is endangered by a compulsion to drink, we need to know that we can leave immediately. We should never allow ourselves to get into a situation where we are trapped. If our last defense against a drink is to leave the setting in which it is offered, we must be able to go. If we cannot guarantee our escape, then we should seriously consider not attending the event.

6. Do I have doubts about going?

"To avoid a slip, avoid slippery places" is an old AA saying. If we have strong doubts about whether to go somewhere, we probably shouldn't go. Our intuition is seldom wrong, and we have gradually learned to trust it. It's better to make a mistake on the side of caution. The price of relapse is very, very high. Sometimes it's fatal.

When in doubt, don't go.

TECHNIQUES FOR PARTIES WHERE ALCOHOL IS BEING SERVED

Many of us have found the following suggestions useful when we attend a party where alcohol is being served:

1. We carry our desire chip or birthday/anniversary chip in our pocket or purse. If necessary, we touch it or hold it to remind ourselves that we don't have to drink again, one day at a time.

2. We take several quarters and the telephone numbers of our sponsors and AA friends, and we call them if we become uneasy or feel that our sobriety is threatened.

**Take quarters and AA telephone
numbers to the party.**

3. We eat before going to the party. We try not to attend a cocktail party on an empty stomach even if food is going to be served there.

**Try not to attend a cocktail
party on an empty stomach.**

4. Especially when we're newly sober, we carry a candy bar to eat if we feel like drinking. Or we drink a milkshake. Experience suggests that a milkshake or a sweet takes the edge off the craving to drink. Alcohol is basically sugar. When we withdraw from alcohol, we often develop a craving for the missing sugar.
5. Upon arriving at the party, we go immediately to the bar and order a drink that contains no alcohol.
6. We always have a glass in our hand—a soft drink, a mineral water, or a similar beverage.
7. We observe that most people don't notice whether we're drinking something alcoholic or not. Normal drinkers are not preoccupied with alcohol or the drinking or not-drinking of it. They couldn't care less.

**At cocktail parties, we always
have a glass in our hands.**

8. If our drink is being poured by someone other than a professional bartender, we watch the person pour it. If our host seems anxious for us to drink, we pour the drink ourselves.

9. We casually smell the drink before tasting it. Our host may be wrong about what we're drinking or may have gotten the order mixed up. Or the bartender may have poured the wrong drink.
10. We hold on to our drinks. We don't leave them on bars or tables where we might later pick up someone else's drink by mistake.
11. Unless we are absolutely certain that it's our drink, we don't drink it. We order another one instead.
12. If we get uncomfortable at the party *for whatever reason,* we leave.

Smell the drink before tasting it.

At Cocktail Parties We Have to Attend
We use the same techniques listed above when our jobs or family obligations require us to attend a party we would rather avoid. In addition

1. We go to an AA meeting first.
2. We arrive as late as possible and leave as early as we can.
3. We call our sponsor or an AA friend before we go to the party and arrange to call the same person afterward to describe how it went.
4. If we think we might drink, we skip the party and make an excuse the next day. Nothing comes before sobriety, not even a job—especially one where abstinence is not supported. If we lose our sobriety, we'll probably lose the job anyway.

**If our sobriety is endangered,
we leave—no matter what.**

SLIPPERY SITUATIONS

Certain situations have proven to be particularly slippery for those new to sobriety. These situations are described below:

Old Drinking or Drugging Places

Places where we used to drink or use other drugs pose special risks. Conditioning is a powerful force in life. It is better, therefore, to avoid these places. We also try to change as many of the old habits relating to drinking and drug use as possible. For example, we may change the route we take home from work to avoid passing a neighborhood bar, liquor store, or convenience store where we used to buy booze. If the five o'clock whistle signaled the start of our drinking, we go to a five o'clock meeting instead. Or we may hang out at an AA clubhouse until a meeting starts.

**Old drinking places carry special dangers
for us when we're new to recovery.**

Old Drinking or Using Friends

When we enter recovery, it is natural to want to keep our old drinking and using friends. After all, we spent a lot of time and shared many adventures with them. At the same time, we realize that something is different. They're drinking and using and we're not, and some of the old camaraderie is gone. The truth is that we gradually grow apart from our old drinking buddies. Alcohol for the alcoholic is the most important thing in life. Life, in fact, centers around the drug. When we quit drinking and our drinking friends continue to drink too much, we have lost our shared focus. The disease of alcoholism continues to consume them, but we are set free.

**Old drinking friends who are still
drinking can be slippery.**

Holiday Parties

Holidays are difficult times for many people. They can be especially difficult for newly recovering alcoholics who find themselves lonely and with many regrets during this "joyous" season. We are careful about attending drinking parties if our mood is not good. When we're feeling depressed or angry or lonely, we don't go where drinking will be emphasized unless we go with someone in recovery.

The first holidays in sobriety are often the most difficult. We stay close to our friends in Alcoholics Anonymous and take advantage of the parties that many AA clubs have. We increase our Twelve Step meetings and try to work with others in recovery. One good thing about the holidays is that there is always an AA meeting somewhere—even on Christmas day.

Stay close to the Fellowship during the holidays.

Toasts

At weddings, dinners, and other occasions where a toast is called for, toast with a glass of water. Active alcoholics are more interested in their own drinks than in yours. Everyone else will be more interested in the object of the toast than in what you're drinking. In other words, whether or not you're drinking is less important to everyone else than it is to you. We are not, after all, the center of attention in a toast to someone else!

Few will notice that the toast is with water and not champagne.

Wine Glasses at Dinners and Restaurants

When we don't want to drink wine at a restaurant or a seated dinner, we can signal that wish to the server by turning our wine glass upside down. The server will remove the glass, and wine will not be served. We can also cover the top of the wine glass when the server comes to pour the wine, and he or she will not pour any. The glass, however, will remain on the table.

**Cover the wine glass or turn it upside
down to signal that no wine is desired.**

AA PARTIES

When we think of having fun, we often think of parties. The safest party for a newcomer is a recovery party. There are lots of them, all solidly in the AA tradition. AA partying began in the 1930s with the founding of the Fellowship. "AA members, and then groups in Akron, began giving parties regularly, including an annual one on Mother's Day to celebrate the meeting of Dr. Bob and Bill Wilson."[3] Henrietta D., an early Akron member, recalled, "We had covered-dish suppers and picnics, and later we had a few dances. Every year, there was a New Year's party at the Y. . . . Everybody was so happy to be together."[4]

**AA partying started along with
the Fellowship—and hasn't stopped!**

Parties are organized by AA groups, local Intergroup/Central Offices, and individuals in a party mood. Potluck suppers, seated dinners, birthday/anniversary celebrations, coffees, dances, pool parties, and "cocktail" parties without the cocktails are staples of Twelve Step recovery entertainment.

Affiliates of the National Council on Alcoholism and Drug Dependence often have holiday parties that emphasize the holiday spirit without the spirits. Various state and regional AA conventions offer weekends filled with meetings and fun and parties. It is even possible to take a "sober vacation" to Club Med where all the vacationers will be in recovery.

**What a surprise it was to learn that
we could have fun in sobriety.**

NEW THINGS TO DO

As we get and stay sober, we learn to party in new ways. The world itself becomes more fascinating. We may take up old hobbies or find new ones. We may enjoy long walks or looking at houses or visiting museums or taking a class or woodworking or gardening or studying a self-improvement course. We may return to old sports or adopt new ones, begin physical training or take up swimming.

The idea of partying expands beyond the walls of a bar. Movies, the theater, concerts may beckon to us. An amusement park or the zoo—activities long lost to us in our drinking days—call out to the child within. We are free again to taste life, to savor its diversity, to relish its beauty.

**There is more to life,
it turns out, than alcohol.**

And we are no longer alone. The essence of the AA Fellowship is, well, fellowship. It is a "we" program of recovery that counters the alcoholic's isolation. There is so much to do with others, from large-scale partying to one-on-one lunches. The opportunities are almost limitless.

Having fun is part of being sober.

For some people, having fun comes naturally. For some entering recovery, however, it seems more like work. It's a decision that has to be made. So make the decision. Honor the child within and rediscover the joy of spontaneity and friendship. Remember what we learned a long time ago as children: nothing beats having fun, especially with friends.

PART 5

APPENDICES

Appendix A

A Brief History of Alcoholics Anonymous

Alcoholics Anonymous was founded in the summer of 1935 by Bill Wilson, a New York investment analyst, and Dr. Robert Smith, an Akron, Ohio, physician. How these two men came to start the AA Fellowship is one of the great stories of the twentieth century.

AA was founded in 1935 by Bill Wilson and Dr. Bob Smith

Bill Wilson was bright, creative, and a born salesman. He was also an alcoholic who suffered from alcoholic grandiosity and serious depression. He was born on November 26, 1895, in East Dorset, Vermont, in a room behind a bar[1] and died on January 24, 1971. Although Bill never graduated from college, he earned a law degree studying nights at the Brooklyn Law School, a division of St. Lawrence University, graduating in 1924. "After paying the fifteen-dollar fee for his diploma, he was too drunk to leave the apartment the next day to pick it up. He never bothered to get it."[2] Nor did he ever practice law. Bill's profession is generally referred to as "stockbroker," but he actually pioneered investment analysis.

Dr. Robert Smith is affectionately called "Dr. Bob" in the AA Fellowship. He was born on August 8, 1879, in St. Johnsbury, Vermont, and died on November 16, 1950. Dr. Bob graduated from Dartmouth College and from the Rush Medical School in Chicago after many problems with alcohol. He was a well-respected and

137

capable proctologist and rectal surgeon (when sober) whose temperament and outlook balanced those of Bill Wilson, his cofounder and sponsor.[3]

Dr. Bob was "the steady hand that held the cord of Bill Wilson's high-flying, erratic kite. While Bill was impulsive, Dr. Bob was deliberate and cautious. He was the soul of common sense."[4] The two men were complementary, and together well suited to the task of building the AA Fellowship. Perhaps it was inevitable that AA would have cofounders rather than a single founder because the essence of the Fellowship is one alcoholic sharing honestly with another.[5]

The two AA cofounders were a good balance for each other.

By 1934, Bill Wilson was in deep trouble with his alcoholism. During the fall of the previous year, he had been admitted to Towns Hospital for alcoholism treatment.[6] Towns Hospital at 293 Central Park West in New York was a fashionable (and expensive) drying-out place. Neither his first stay nor two subsequent treatments worked. By now, Bill was basically unemployable. His physician had told his wife that he was hopeless and would very likely have to be put away permanently.

Such was Bill's situation when an old boyhood friend, Ebby Thatcher, dropped by one November day in 1934.[7] The two men met across the table in the kitchen of Bill's home on Clinton Street in Brooklyn, New York.[8] Ebby had heard of Bill's desperate situation and brought news of how he had gotten sober just in time to keep from being committed to an asylum.

Ebby told Bill about Calvary Episcopal Mission and the Oxford Groups that met there. He told him about how he had gotten sober attending meetings of the Oxford Group, a spiritual, nondenominational movement. He urged Bill to join the group. One afternoon in early December 1934, a drunk Bill Wilson went to investigate the mission and stayed for a meeting that night.[9] Because of that meeting,

Bill decided, two or three days later, to reenter Towns Hospital. He returned to the hospital on December 11, 1934 (for the fourth and last time).[10]

Ebby T. told Bill how he had gotten sober in the Oxford Group and urged him to join.

It was during this last hospital stay that Bill had the spiritual experience that transformed his life. (Appendix C has a description of that experience.) After the experience, he sought the advice of Dr. William Silkworth, the hospital's medical director. Dr. Silkworth assured Bill that he was not insane and suggested that he read William James' *Varieties of Religious Experience*. Dr. Silkworth also told Bill that he believed that alcoholism was a physical allergy to alcohol combined with a mental obsession and a compulsion to drink. This concept of alcoholism as a disease rather than as a moral failure or lack of willpower was a radical one for the 1930s. It became a fundamental part of the AA approach to recovery.

It was in Towns Hospital that Bill Wilson had his spiritual experience.

Bill was released from Towns Hospital on December 18, 1934, and began attending Oxford Group meetings regularly in an effort to stay sober.[11] The Oxford Group was founded in 1921 by a Lutheran minister, Dr. Frank Buchman. Dr. Buchman had "perfected methods of meeting in small groups and sharing experiences in order to practice personal honesty and help others in their growth and change. . . . He achieved early success in helping alcoholics recover. . . ."[12] Bill Wilson wrote that "early A.A. got its ideas of self-examination, acknowledgment of character defects, restitution for harm done, and working with others straight from the Oxford Groups. . . ."[13]

While a member of the Oxford Group, Bill began working intensively with other alcoholics. During the first months of his sobriety in

1935, however, he was unable to get a single person sober. Dr. Silkworth told Bill that his problem was "preaching" to the alcoholic and talking too much about his spiritual experience. The doctor suggested that Bill talk about the illness of alcoholism instead.[14] "For God's sake stop preaching," Dr. Silkworth advised Bill. "You're scaring the poor drunks half crazy."[15]

Dr. Silkworth called alcoholism "an allergy to alcohol," not a moral weakness or lack of willpower.

About this time, Bill went on a business trip to Akron, Ohio. The day before Mother's Day in 1935, Bill Wilson found himself stranded at the Mayflower Hotel. It was a hot Saturday afternoon, and he had only ten dollars in his pocket. The proxy fight that had brought him to Akron had failed, his friends had returned to New York City, and he stood alone in the hotel lobby considering his next move. He had not had a drink since his spiritual experience in Towns Hospital five months earlier.[16]

Bill "began to pace the lobby, from the elevators past the manager's desk to a row of telephones, then back along the same route. Directly across from his path of march was the entrance to the Mayflower Bar, and with every step he took he was growing more aware of the cool inviting darkness just beyond the entrance, the low din of male voices, occasionally interrupted by a girl's happy laugh, or the sweet crackling sound of ice in a cocktail shaker. Then came—as he may have always known they would—the words: Why not? Who would know? And what harm could one drink do?

"Instantly he panicked. He felts his knees go weak; a cold sweat ran down his arms. . . . There was one thing he knew he had to do—and do immediately. As he'd been pacing out his beat, he'd been aware of a glass-enclosed sign, a sort of bulletin, beside the telephones. His eye had passed over this, hardly noticing it, but he had the impression it was a church directory. He walked back and stood for a long moment, studying the names of churches, ministers and times of services. Then choosing one name at random, Reverend Walter Tunks, he stepped into the booth and made a call."[17]

**It was in the lobby of the
Mayflower Hotel that Bill Wilson
made the telephone call that ultimately
led him to a meeting with Dr. Bob.**

Through Reverend Tunks, Bill contacted Henrietta Seiberling. Henrietta was a nonalcoholic, an Oxford Group member, and a close friend of Dr. Bob's. She had been trying without success to get Dr. Bob sober through the Oxford Group. Bill asked her to help him find another alcoholic he could work with and described himself as a "rum hound from New York." She immediately suggested Dr. Bob as the other alcoholic. Unfortunately, Dr. Bob was too drunk to meet anybody that day. So the meeting with Bill was scheduled for the following afternoon.

It was in the gatehouse of the Seiberling estate that Dr. Bob and Bill Wilson met on May 12, 1935.[18] Dr. Bob arrived at 5 P.M. with his wife and seventeen-year-old son, intending to stay no more than fifteen minutes. His conversation with Bill lasted for six and one-quarter hours.[19] Bill followed Dr. Silkworth's advice and talked to Dr. Bob about the disease of alcoholism. At the time of their meeting, Bill had been a member of the New York Oxford Group for five months and Dr. Bob a member of the Akron Oxford Group for two and a half years.[20]

**Both Bill Wilson and Dr. Bob
were members of the Oxford
Group when they met.**

Although Dr. Bob drank again after that meeting, he got sober on June 10, 1935. AA dates its founding from Dr. Bob's last drink.

Within two days of that date, Bill and Dr. Bob had made their first Twelfth Step call on a hospital patient who became AA's third member. AA expanded in Akron under Dr. Bob's guidance and in New York under Bill's and later separated from the Oxford Group.[21]

The remarkable story of how AA grew from two men meeting in Akron to two million men and women meeting all over the world is contained in three Conference-approved books:

- *Alcoholics Anonymous Comes of Age: A Brief History of A.A.*
- *'Pass It On,' The Story of Bill Wilson and How the A.A. Message Reached the World*
- *Dr. Bob and the Good Oldtimers: A Biography, with Recollections of Early A.A. in the Midwest*

Appendix B

The Big Book

*A*lcoholics Anonymous, AA's basic textbook, is affectionately referred to as the "Big Book." This appendix is about how it came to be written.

**The Fellowship of Alcoholics Anonymous
took its name from the book *Alcoholics
Anonymous*, not vice versa.**

PURPOSE OF THE BIG BOOK

The small groups of recovering alcoholics started by Bill Wilson and Dr. Bob still didn't have a name in the fall of 1937. Their numbers had grown to forty people—twenty had been sober more than a year.[1] All of them had been diagnosed as hopeless cases until their recovery through the Fellowship. Awed by their own sobriety, they wanted to spread the news to as many other alcoholics as possible.

The members of early AA depended on word of mouth to explain their recovery program to newcomers. As AA began to grow, its members realized that a book would also help them reach more people. A book that specifically described how their method of recovery worked would also prevent the program from being distorted by the continuous retelling.[2] According to the foreword to the first edition of the Big Book, "To show other alcoholics *precisely how we have recovered* is the main purpose of this book."

**The purpose of the Big Book was to describe
exactly how the first one hundred members
of AA recovered from alcoholism.**

143

THE AUTHOR AND THE WRITING PROCESS

Bill Wilson wrote the first eleven chapters of the Big Book. He started working on it in the spring of 1938. Bill dictated most of the book to Ruth Hock, Hank P.'s secretary, from notes written on yellow legal pads. Hank's office at 17 William Street, Newark, New Jersey, served as AA's first office from 1937 until 1939.[3]

**Bill Wilson is the author of the Big Book
(except for the personal stories in the back).**

Robert Thomsen, Bill Wilson's biographer, records that "there was remarkable timing in Bill's starting to write exactly when he did. It was as though it threw an inner switch that had been waiting to be thrown for years. He'd been sober for some time, but he was still close enough to the raw emotions and suffering, the self-loathing, the terrors, to be able to call them up and present the ugly facts of the obsession that had ruled his life and that finally had placed him beyond any human help. In 1938 he was in direct touch with all the simple truths that had been guiding him since his first meeting with Dr. Bob."[4]

Bill wrote during the day, then read what he had written to the members of the Clinton Street meeting at night. After they had discussed the chapter ("going over every detail and making suggestions"), Bill sent it to Akron for the opinions of members there.[5] He listened to comments and criticisms, defended his work, and sometimes rewrote it.

**Bill revised the book based on suggestions
from AA members in New York and Akron.**

Then Bill came to chapter 5. It was here that he wanted to explain exactly how the program of recovery worked. "Ever since he and Bob had tried to shape a program, their ideas had been based on Oxford Group principles: first admitting they were powerless over alcohol, then making a moral inventory, confessing their shortcomings to another, making amends whenever possible, and finally praying for the power to carry out these concepts and to help other drunks. This had been their word-of-mouth program. But now, putting it on paper, Bill felt a need to pin it down in specific steps, so that there could be no questions in the reader's mind, no possible loopholes through which the rationalizing alcoholic could wiggle away."[6]

One night in late December 1938, Bill lay in bed at his home on Clinton Street in Brooklyn, New York. He had a pencil in his hand and a tablet of scratch paper on his knee. It was time to write the steps of the program. This is how he describes doing it: "Finally I started to write. I set out to draft more than six steps; how many more I did not know. I relaxed and asked for guidance. With a speed that was astonishing, considering my jangling emotions, I completed the first draft. It took perhaps half an hour. The words kept right on coming. When I reached a stopping point, I numbered the new steps. They added up to twelve. Somehow this number seemed significant."[7]

> ### Bill Wilson turned AA's early word-of-mouth program into the Twelve Steps, writing them in about half an hour.

The Twelve Steps as Bill originally wrote them created a violent reaction among group members. The central problem was God. The conservatives in the group wanted to write frankly of Christian concepts. The liberals were willing to write of spiritual concepts and even to mention God, but with a strong psychological basis. The radicals (the atheists and agnostics) wanted the word "God" excluded.[8] Bill worked to reach a compromise among the opposing sides, and the Steps were finally approved by the groups in a slightly different form.

Bill Wilson writes, "Who first suggested the actual compromise words I do not know, but they are words well known throughout the length and breadth of A.A. today: In Step Two we decided to describe God as a 'Power greater than ourselves.' In Steps Three and Eleven we inserted the words 'God *as we understood Him.*' From Step Seven we deleted the expression 'on our knees.' And, as a lead-in sentence to all the steps we wrote these words: 'Here are the steps we took which are suggested as a Program of Recovery.' A.A.'s Twelve Steps were to be *suggestions* only."[9]

"Bill saw that those italicized words ["*as we understood Him*" after the word "God"] would not only widen the gateway so that all drunks could pass through, regardless of their belief or lack of belief. In time they might also force many men to come to terms with what they understood God to be, with what it was in their lives that they truly believed in."[10]

A compromise added the phrase "as we understood Him" to the word "God" in the Twelve Steps.

Case histories for the stories section of the Big Book were sought from the Akron and the New York groups. "By the end of January 1939, the manuscript was ready for preliminary distribution; 400 copies were Multilithed and circulated to members, friends, and other allies for comments and evaluation."[11] Doctors and ministers were included in this review process to help find errors and spot objection-able material.

PROPOSED TITLES

Alcoholic's [sic] *Anonymous* was the title that Bill Wilson gave the original Multilithed copies. Many members in New York and even more in Akron found the title unacceptable.[12]

Alcoholics Anonymous was initially rejected as a title for the Big Book.

More than one hundred titles were considered including, at Bill's suggestion, *The B. W. Movement* and *The Wilson Movement*, both of which were quickly abandoned.[13] *The Way Out* or *A Way Out*, which emphasized hope, was popular from the start. Other possibilities included *Haven, Comes the Dawn, The Empty Glass, The Dry Way, Dry Frontiers,* and *One Hundred Men by Alcoholics Anonymous.* The last title emphasized that the new organization had been successful in getting people sober, but it did not please the sole woman AA member.[14]

More than one hundred titles were originally considered for the Big Book.

The battle of titles came down to *The Way Out,* favored by the Akron group, and *Alcoholics Anonymous,* favored by the New York group. When the final vote of AAs was taken, *The Way Out* won by a bare majority. Bill Wilson favored the losing title and had an AA member check out both titles in the Library of Congress. There were twenty-five books entitled *The Way Out* and none entitled *Alcoholics Anonymous.* On that basis, the latter name was chosen.[15]

EARLY REVIEWS

The first reactions to the mimeographed copies of the book were favorable. Protestant ministers and Catholic priests as well as medical men and psychiatrists approved of the new book. Not all of the reviews were favorable, however. The *Journal of the American Medical Association* of October 14, 1939, concluded that "The one valid thing in the book is the recognition of the seriousness of addiction to alcohol. Other than this, the book has no scientific merit or interest."[16] Seventeen years later (in 1956) the American Medical Association accepted alcoholism as a "treatable illness" and in 1972 recognized it as a "disease."[17]

"Some manuscript readers sent in very helpful ideas, such as: 'Make it more personal by using the pronoun 'we' instead of 'you'; 'Change the musts for getting sober into suggestions; no one likes musts'; 'Change the past tense to the present.'"[18] These suggestions were followed, and then the manuscript was sent to Tom U., a writer for *Collier's* magazine, to be "sharpened."[19]

**Many early reviews of the
Big Book were favorable.**

HOW THE NICKNAME DEVELOPED

The Big Book was finally published in April 1939 on very thick paper to convince buyers that they were getting their money's worth at $3.50 a copy. The book was quite large and very bulky and was laughingly referred to as the "big book." It was half an inch thicker than the current hardback although it contained less copy and fourteen fewer personal stories.[20]

**The Big Book got its name from its size
which was caused by thick paper.**

PUBLISHING HISTORY AND THE THIRD EDITION

Over 300,000 copies of the first edition of the Big Book went into circulation.[21] The second edition was published in July 1955. The original first eleven chapters that described the AA recovery program were almost unchanged. More stories of women, younger members, and AAs with "high bottoms" were added to the stories section.[22] Over 1,150,000 copies entered circulation.[23]

The third edition of the Big Book was published in 1976. No changes were made except to the stories section. As of May 1994, over thirteen and one-half million copies of the third edition were in circulation, bringing the total number of Big Books to more than fifteen million.[24] The Big Book has been translated into twenty-nine languages.

**Over fifteen million Big Books
have been distributed since 1939.**

Appendix C

Often Quoted Passages

This appendix contains the complete text of some of the passages that are often quoted in Alcoholics Anonymous meetings. Each quotation includes the original source.

AA PREAMBLE

Alcoholics Anonymous is a fellowship of men and women who share their experience, strength and hope with each other that they may solve their common problem and help others to recover from alcoholism.

The only requirement for membership is a desire to stop drinking. There are no dues or fees for A.A. membership; we are self-supporting through our own contributions. A.A. is not allied with any sect, denomination, politics, organization or institution; does not wish to engage in any controversy; neither endorses nor opposes any causes. Our primary purpose is to stay sober and help other alcoholics to achieve sobriety.

The Preamble is based on a portion of the foreword to the first edition of the Big Book. It was "first formulated by an A.A. Grapevine *editor in 1946."*[1]

AA PROMISES

If we are painstaking about this phase of our development, we will be amazed before we are half way through. We are going to know a new freedom and a new happiness. We will not regret the past nor wish to shut the door on it. We will comprehend the word serenity and we will know peace. No matter how far down the scale we have gone, we will see how our experience can benefit others. That feeling of uselessness and self-pity will disappear. We will lose interest in selfish things and gain interest in our fellows. Self-seeking will slip away. Our whole attitude and outlook upon life will change. Fear of people and of economic insecurity will leave us. We will intuitively know how to handle situations which used to baffle us. We will suddenly realize that God is doing for us what we could not do for ourselves.

Are these extravagant promises? We think not. They are being fulfilled among us—sometimes quickly, sometimes slowly. They will always materialize if we work for them.

The Promises are taken from chapter 6 of the Big Book, pages 83–84.

A VISION FOR YOU

We realize we know only a little. God will constantly disclose more to you and to us. Ask Him in your morning meditation what you can do each day for the man who is still sick. The answers will come, if your own house is in order. But obviously you cannot transmit something you haven't got. See to it that your relationship with Him is right, and great events will come to pass for you and countless others. This is the Great Fact for us.

Abandon yourself to God as you understand God. Admit your faults to Him and to your fellows. Clear away the wreckage of your past. Give freely of what you find and join us. We shall be with you in the Fellowship of the Spirit, and you will surely meet some of us as you trudge the Road of Happy Destiny.

May God bless you and keep you—until then.

A Vision for You appears in chapter 11 of the Big Book, page 164.

BILL WILSON'S SPIRITUAL EXPERIENCE

Bill Wilson had a spiritual *experience* that changed his life. Dr. Bob had a spiritual *awakening* that changed his life. Bill's spiritual experience "gave him a belief in God, or Higher Power, that never wavered despite much suffering in later years, including a recurring profound depression." As Bill put it in a 1956 letter:

With me, the original experience was so prodigious, the preview of destiny so intense, that I have never had any difficulty with doubts since that time. Even at my worst, and that has often been damn bad, the sense of the presence of God has never deserted me. . . . Never has there been any question about the ultimate destiny of us all, or of God's justice and love.[2]

The following is a description of Bill Wilson's spiritual experience as he described it in *'Pass It On:' The Story of Bill Wilson and How the A.A. Message Reached the World.*

In a few days, Ebby visited him [in Towns Hospital]. Again, they talked as they had at the kitchen table [when Ebby explained to Bill about his recovery in the Oxford Group]. Ebby's visit made Bill momentarily less depressed, but after Ebby left, Bill slid into a very deep melancholy. He was filled with guilt and remorse over the way he had treated Lois [his wife], Lois who had stood by him unwavering throughout. He thought about the miraculous moments they had shared standing on the Newport cliffs the night before he sailed for England, the camping trips, the wonderful years as motorcycle bums, the triumphs and failures on Wall Street. He thought about Winchester Cathedral, and the moment he had almost believed in God.

Now, he and Lois were waiting for the end. Now, there was nothing ahead but death or madness. This was the finish, the jumping-off place. "The terrifying darkness had become complete," Bill said. "In agony of spirit, I again thought of the cancer of alcoholism which had now consumed me in mind and spirit, and soon the body." The abyss gaped before him.

In his helplessness and desperation, Bill cried out, "I'll do anything, anything at all!" He had reached a point of total, utter deflation—a state of complete absolute surrender. With neither faith nor hope, he cried, "If there be a God, let Him show Himself!"

What happened next was electric. "Suddenly, my room blazed with an indescribably white light. I was seized with an ecstasy beyond description. Every joy I had known was pale by comparison. The light, the ecstasy—I was conscious of nothing else for a time.

"Then, seen in the mind's eye, there was a mountain. I stood upon its summit, where a great wind blew. A wind, not of air, but of spirit. In great, clean strength, it blew right through me. Then came the blazing thought 'You are a free man.' I know not at all how long I remained in this state, but finally the light and the ecstasy subsided. I again saw the wall of my room. As I became more quiet, a great peace stole over me, and this was accompanied by a sensation difficult to describe. I became acutely conscious of a Presence which seemed like a veritable sea of living spirit. I lay on the shores of a new world. 'This,' I thought, 'must be the great reality. The God of the preachers.'

"Savoring my new world, I remained in this state for a long time. I seemed to be possessed by the absolute, and the curious conviction deepened that no matter how wrong things seemed to be, there could be no question of the ultimate rightness of God's universe. For the first time, I felt that I really belonged. I knew that I was loved and could love in return. I thanked my God, who had given me a glimpse of His absolute self. Even though a pilgrim upon an uncertain highway, I need be concerned no more, for I had glimpsed the great beyond."

Bill Wilson had just had his 39th birthday, and he still had half his life ahead of him. He always said that after that experience, he never again doubted the existence of God. He never took another drink.[3]

HOW IT WORKS

Rarely have we seen a person fail who has thoroughly followed our path. Those who do not recover are people who cannot or will not completely give themselves to this simple program, usually men and women who are constitutionally incapable of being honest with themselves. There are such unfortunates. They are not at fault; they seem to have been born that way. They are naturally incapable of grasping and developing a manner of living which demands rigorous honesty. Their chances are less than average. There are those, too, who suffer from grave emotional and mental disorders, but many of them do recover if they have the capacity to be honest.

Our stories disclose in a general way what we used to be like, what happened, and what we are like now. If you have decided you want what we have and are willing to go to any length to get it—then you are ready to take certain steps.

At some of these we balked. We thought we could find an easier, softer way. But we could not. With all the earnestness at our command, we beg of you to be fearless and thorough from the very start. Some of us have tried to hold on to our old ideas and the result was nil until we let go absolutely.

Remember that we deal with alcohol—cunning, baffling, powerful! Without help it is too much for us. But there is One who has all power—that One is God. May you find Him now!

Half measures availed us nothing. We stood at the turning point. We asked His protection and care with complete abandon.

Here are the steps we took, which are suggested as a program of recovery:

1. We admitted we were powerless over alcohol—that our lives had become unmanageable.
2. Came to believe that a Power greater than ourselves could restore us to sanity.
3. Made a decision to turn our will and our lives over to the care of God *as we understood Him.*
4. Made a searching and fearless moral inventory of ourselves.
5. Admitted to God, to ourselves, and to another human being the exact nature of our wrongs.
6. Were entirely ready to have God remove all these defects of character.
7. Humbly asked Him to remove our shortcomings.
8. Made a list of all persons we had harmed, and became willing to make amends to them all.
9. Made direct amends to such people wherever possible, except when to do so would injure them or others.
10. Continued to take personal inventory and when we were wrong promptly admitted it.
11. Sought through prayer and meditation to improve our conscious contact with God *as we understood Him,* praying only for knowledge of His will for us and the power to carry that out.
12. Having had a spiritual awakening as the result of these steps, we tried to carry this message to alcoholics, and to practice these principles in all our affairs.

Many of us exclaimed, "What an order! I can't go through with it." Do not be discouraged. No one among us has been able to maintain anything like perfect adherence to these principles. We are not saints. The point is, that we are willing to grow along spiritual lines. The principles we have set down are guides to progress. We claim spiritual progress rather than spiritual perfection.

Our description to the alcoholic, the chapter to the agnostic, and our personal adventures before and after make clear three pertinent ideas:

(a) That we were alcoholic and could not manage our own lives.
(b) That probably no human power could have relieved our alcoholism.
(c) That God could and would if He were sought.

How It Works is found in chapter 5 of the Big Book, pages 58–60. The first two and one-half pages quoted here are sometimes read at the beginning of AA meetings and are referred to as "How It Works."

PRAYER OF ST. FRANCIS OF ASSISI (ELEVENTH STEP PRAYER)

Lord, make me a channel of thy peace—
That where there is hatred, I may bring love—
That where there is wrong, I may bring the spirit of forgiveness—
That where there is discord, I may bring harmony—
That where there is error, I may bring truth—
That where there is doubt, I may bring faith—
That where there is despair, I may bring hope—
That where there are shadows, I may bring light—
That where there is sadness, I may bring joy.
Lord, grant that I may seek
Rather to comfort than to be comforted—
To understand, than to be understood—
To love, than to be loved.
For it is by self-forgetting that one finds.
It is by forgiving that one is forgiven.
It is by dying that one awakens to Eternal Life. Amen

Soon after they met, Bill Wilson's spiritual advisor, Father Ed Dowling, gave him a copy of this prayer.[4] It is quoted in "Step Eleven" in Twelve Steps and Twelve Traditions, *page 99.*

RESPONSIBILITY DECLARATION

I am responsible. When anyone, anywhere, reaches out for help, I want the hand of AA always to be there. And for that: I am responsible.

The Responsibility Declaration was adopted at the AA International Convention in 1965.

SERENITY PRAYER

God, grant me the serenity to accept the things I cannot change, the courage to change the things I can, and the wisdom to know the difference.

The Serenity Prayer "is usually credited to Reinhold Niebuhr, a 20th-century theologian, who in turn credited an 18th-century theologian, Friedrich Oetinger."[5]

SEVENTH STEP PRAYER

My Creator, I am now willing that you should have all of me, good and bad. I pray that you now remove from me every single defect of character which stands in the way of my usefulness to you and my fellows. Grant me strength, as I go out from here, to do your bidding. Amen.

The Seventh Step Prayer relates to AA's Seventh Step and is taken from chapter 7 of the Big Book, page 76.

SINGLENESS OF PURPOSE STATEMENT

For a Closed Meeting

This is a *closed* meeting of Alcoholics Anonymous. In support of A.A.'s singleness of purpose, attendance at closed meetings is limited to persons who have a desire to stop drinking. If you think you have a problem with alcohol, you are welcome to attend this meeting. We ask that when discussing problems, we confine ourselves to those problems as they relate to alcohol.

For an Open Meeting

This is an *open* meeting of Alcoholics Anonymous. We are glad you are all here—especially newcomers. In keeping with our singleness of purpose and our Third Tradition which states that "The only requirement of A.A. membership is a desire to stop drinking," we ask that all who participate confine their discussion to their problems with alcohol.

Advisory Actions of the 1987 General Service Conference made official these singleness of purpose statements that can be read at AA meetings.

THIRD STEP PRAYER

God, I offer myself to Thee—to build with me and to do with me as Thou wilt. Relieve me of the bondage of self, that I may better do Thy will. Take away my difficulties, that victory over them may bear witness to those I would help of Thy Power, Thy Love, and Thy Way of life. May I do Thy will always!

The Third Step Prayer relates to AA's Third Step and is taken from chapter five of the Big Book, page 63.

TWELVE STEPS OF ALCOHOLICS ANONYMOUS

1. We admitted we were powerless over alcohol—that our lives had become unmanageable.
2. Came to believe that a Power greater than ourselves could restore us to sanity.
3. Made a decision to turn our will and our lives over to the care of God *as we understood Him.*
4. Made a searching and fearless moral inventory of ourselves.
5. Admitted to God, to ourselves, and to another human being the exact nature of our wrongs.
6. Were entirely ready to have God remove all these defects of character.
7. Humbly asked Him to remove our shortcomings.
8. Made a list of all persons we had harmed, and became willing to make amends to them all.
9. Made direct amends to such people wherever possible, except when to do so would injure them or others.
10. Continued to take personal inventory and when we were wrong promptly admitted it.
11. Sought through prayer and meditation to improve our conscious contact with God *as we understood Him,* praying only for knowledge of His will for us and the power to carry that out.
12. Having had a spiritual awakening as the result of these steps, we tried to carry this message to alcoholics, and to practice these principles in all our affairs.

The Twelve Steps appear in the Big Book, pages 59-60.

TWELVE TRADITIONS OF ALCOHOLICS ANONYMOUS (SHORT FORM)

1. Our common welfare should come first; personal recovery depends upon A.A. unity.
2. For our group purpose there is but one ultimate authority—a loving God as He may express Himself in our group conscience. Our leaders are but trusted servants; they do not govern.
3. The only requirement for A.A. membership is a desire to stop drinking.
4. Each group should be autonomous except in matters affecting other groups or A.A. as a whole.
5. Each group has but one primary purpose—to carry its message to the alcoholic who still suffers.

6. An A.A. group ought never endorse, finance, or lend the A.A. name to any related facility or outside enterprise, lest problems of money, property, and prestige divert us from our primary purpose.

7. Every A.A. group ought to be fully self-supporting, declining outside contributions.

8. Alcoholics Anonymous should remain forever nonprofessional, but our service centers may employ special workers.

9. A.A., as such, ought never be organized; but we may create service boards or committees directly responsible to those they serve.

10. Alcoholics Anonymous has no opinion on outside issues; hence the A.A. name ought never be drawn into public controversy.

11. Our public relations policy is based on attraction rather than promotion; we need always maintain personal anonymity at the level of press, radio, and films.

12. Anonymity is the spiritual foundation of all our traditions, ever reminding us to place principles before personalities.

The Traditions were first published in the "long form" in the A.A. *Grapevine of May 6, 1946 and were later confirmed at AA's First International Convention held in Cleveland, Ohio in 1950. Bill Wilson writes, "We saw that the A.A. Traditions were the key to the unity, the functioning, and even the survival of Alcoholics Anonymous. In reality I had not been the author of the Traditions at all. I had merely put them on paper in such a way as to mirror principles which had already been developed in A.A. group experience."*[6]

The Traditions "are little else than a list of sacrifices which the experience of twenty years has taught us that we must make, individually and collectively, if A.A. itself is to stay alive and healthy."[7]

Twelve Traditions of Alcoholics Anonymous (Long Form)

Our A.A. experience has taught us that:

1. Each member of Alcoholics Anonymous is but a small part of a great whole. A.A. must continue to live or most of us will surely die. Hence our common welfare comes first. But individual welfare follows close afterward.

2. For our group purpose there is but one ultimate authority—a loving God as He may express Himself in our group conscience.

3. Our membership ought to include all who suffer from alcoholism. Hence we may refuse none who wish to recover. Nor ought A.A. membership ever depend upon money or conformity. Any two or three alcoholics gathered together for sobriety may

call themselves an A.A. group, provided that, as a group, they have no other affiliation.

4. With respect to its own affairs, each A.A. group should be responsible to no other authority than its own conscience. But when its plans concern the welfare of neighboring groups also, those groups ought to be consulted. And no group, regional committee, or individual should ever take any action that might greatly affect A.A. as a whole without conferring with the trustees of the General Service Board. On such issues our common welfare is paramount.

5. Each Alcoholics Anonymous group ought to be a spiritual entity *having but one primary purpose*—that of carrying its message to the alcoholic who still suffers.

6. Problems of money, property, and authority may easily divert us from our primary spiritual aim. We think, therefore, that any considerable property of genuine use to A.A. should be separately incorporated and managed, thus dividing the material from the spiritual. An A.A. group, as such, should never go into business. Secondary aids to A.A., such as clubs or hospitals which require much property or administration, ought to be incorporated and so set apart that, if necessary, they can be freely discarded by the groups. Hence such facilities ought not to use the A.A. name. Their management should be the sole responsibility of those people who financially support them. For clubs, A.A. managers are usually preferred. But hospitals, as well as other places of recuperation, ought to be well outside A.A.—and medically supervised. While an A.A. group may cooperate with anyone, such cooperation ought never to go so far as affiliation or endorsement, actual or implied. An A.A. group can bind itself to no one.

7. The A.A. groups themselves ought to be fully supported by the voluntary contributions of their own members. We think that each group should soon achieve this ideal; that any public solicitation of funds using the name of Alcoholics Anonymous is highly dangerous, whether by groups, clubs, hospitals, or other outside agencies; that acceptance of large gifts from any source, or of contributions carrying any obligation whatever, is unwise. Then, too, we view with much concern those A.A. treasuries which continue, beyond prudent reserves, to accumulate funds for no stated A.A. purpose. Experience has often warned us that nothing can so surely destroy our spiritual heritage as futile disputes over property, money, and authority.

8. Alcoholics Anonymous should remain forever nonprofessional. We define professionalism as the occupation of counseling alcoholics for fees or hire. But we may employ alcoholics where they are going to perform those services for which we might otherwise have to engage nonalcoholics. Such special services may be well recompensed. But our usual A.A. Twelfth Step work is never to be paid for.

9. Each A.A. group needs the least possible organization. Rotating leadership is the best. The small group may elect its secretary, the large group its rotating committee, and the groups of a large metropolitan area their central or intergroup committee, which often employs a full-time secretary. The trustees of the General Service Board are, in effect, our A.A. General Service Committee. They are the custodians of our A.A. Tradition and the receivers of voluntary A.A. contributions by which we maintain our A.A. General Service Office at New York. They are authorized by the groups to handle our overall public relations and they guarantee the integrity of our principal newspaper, the *A.A. Grapevine.* All such representatives are to be guided in the spirit of service, for true leaders in A.A. are but trusted and experienced servants of the whole. They derive no real authority from their titles; they do not govern. Universal respect is the key to their usefulness.

10. No A.A. group or member should ever, in such a way as to implicate A.A., express any opinion on outside controversial issues—particularly those of politics, alcohol reform, or sectarian religion. The Alcoholics Anonymous groups oppose no one. Concerning such matters they can express no views whatever.

11. Our relations with the general public should be characterized by personal anonymity. We think A.A. ought to avoid sensational advertising. Our names and pictures as A.A. members ought not be broadcast, filmed, or publicly printed. Our public relations should be guided by the principle of attraction rather than promotion. There is never need to praise ourselves. We feel it better to let our friends recommend us.

12. And finally, we of Alcoholics Anonymous believe that the principle of anonymity has an immense spiritual significance. It reminds us that we are to place principles before personalities; that we are actually to practice a genuine humility. This to the end that our great blessings may never spoil us; that we shall forever live in thankful contemplation of Him who presides over us all.

Appendix D

Other Books about AA

There are two categories of books about Alcoholics Anonymous: Conference-approved and nonconference-approved. The term "Conference-approved" refers to literature that has been approved for publication by the AA General Service Conference. It includes both books and pamphlets. Since AA "neither endorses nor opposes any causes" and "has no opinion on outsides issues," all AA literature must adhere to these strict guidelines. Conference-approved literature contains information that is in line with AA traditions. This book, for example, is not Conference-approved and does not officially represent the views of AA.

> **Conference-approved literature refers to books and pamphlets that have been approved for publication by the AA General Service Conference.**

I have restricted the list of books in this chapter to those about AA itself and to a few that are now of historical interest. Together, they make up a basic library. I have not included the large number of pamphlets available from AA. Nor have I included books on meditation (except the old favorite) or books on how to work the Twelve Steps.

CONFERENCE-APPROVED BOOKS

All Conference-approved books are worth reading. They include the following books, all of which are available from AA World

Services, Inc., Box 459, Grand Central Station, New York, NY 10163. To order the catalog or a book, dial: 1 (212) 870-3312.

1. *Alcoholics Anonymous* (the Big Book), third edition. The basic text of AA. [Hardback or paperback]
2. *Twelve Steps and Twelve Traditions* (the Twelve and Twelve). Bill Wilson's twenty-four essays on the Twelve Steps and the Twelve Traditions of Alcoholics Anonymous. [Hardback or paperback]
3. *Alcoholics Anonymous Comes of Age: A Brief History of A.A.* Bill Wilson tells the story of how AA began and grew, and how the Steps and Traditions developed. [Hardback]
4. *As Bill Sees It.* A collection of Bill Wilson's writings. [Hardback]
5. *Dr. Bob and the Good Oldtimers: A Biography, with Recollections of Early A.A. in the Midwest.* A biography of Dr. Robert Smith ("Dr. Bob"), AA's cofounder. [Hardback]
6. *'Pass It On,' The Story of Bill Wilson and How the A.A. Message Reached the World.* A biography of Bill Wilson, AA's cofounder. [Hardback]
7. *Daily Reflections: A Book of Reflections by A.A. Members for A.A. Members.* A book of readings for each day of the year in which AA members reflect on their favorite quotations from AA literature. [Paperback]
8. *Came to Believe.* A collection of seventy-six brief stories by AA members who describe what AA's phrase "spiritual adventures" has meant to them. [20-page paperback]
9. *Living Sober: Some Methods A.A. Members Have Used for Not Drinking.* A booklet of practical methods AA members throughout the world have used to stay sober one day at a time. [88-page paperback]
10. *A.A. in Prison: Inmate to Inmate.* A collection of thirty-two stories from the *A.A. Grapevine* about men and women who found AA while in prison. [128-page paperback]

NONCONFERENCE-APPROVED BOOKS

The following books have not been approved by the AA General Services Conference, but are well worth reading:

1. *The Language of the Heart: Bill W.'s Grapevine Writings.* This book contains nearly every article written for the *A.A. Grapevine* by Bill Wilson. [410-page hardback. New York: The A.A. Grapevine, Inc., 1988]

2. *Not-God: A History of Alcoholics Anonymous* by Ernest Kurtz. This book, which grew out of Kurtz' Ph.D. dissertation at Harvard University, is probably the single best book ever written on the history of AA. It is thorough, captivating, insightful, and inspiring. [436-page paperback. Center City, Minnesota: Hazelden Educational Materials, 1979 (expanded version, 1991)]

3. *Bill W.* by Robert Thomsen is the unofficial biography of Bill Wilson. [373-page paperback. New York: Perennial Library, a division of Harper & Row Publishers, 1975]

4. *Lois Remembers* by Lois W. An Al-Anon publication in which Lois Wilson, Bill's wife, recalls her life before and after her marriage to Bill Wilson. [204-page hardback. New York: Al-Anon Family Group Headquarters, Inc., 1979]

5. *A New Pair of Glasses* by Chuck C. An old favorite, this touching book by an AA member describes what life was like for him as an active alcoholic, what happened, and what it was like in recovery. [Irvine, California: New-Look Publishing Company, 1984]

6. *New Wine: The Spiritual Roots of the Twelve Step Miracle* by Mel B. Despite its eccentric title, the book does a good job of discussing AA's spiritual roots. [193-page paperback. Center City, Minnesota: Hazelden Foundation, 1991]

7. *Search for Serenity* by Lewis F. Presnall is another old AA favorite. [Salt Lake City, Utah: Utah Alcoholism Foundation, 1959]

8. *Twenty-Four Hours a Day* is the traditional meditation book that reflects the thinking of early AA. It was first published in 1956 and contains one meditation for each day. [Hardback or paperback. Center City, Minnesota: Hazelden Foundation, Inc., 1956 (revised edition copyrighted 1975).]

9. *Sermon on the Mount: The Key to Success in Life* by Emmet Fox is an old-time favorite from the early days of AA (available in paperback). Emmet Fox "was a writer and popular New York minister of the 1930s and 1940s who influenced the pioneering AAs."[1] *Sermon on the Mount* (1934) was one of AAs most important works until publication of the Big Book. It was "required reading for everybody," recalled Dorothy S. M., an AA pioneer. "As soon as men in the hospital could begin to focus their eyes, they got a copy of *Sermon on the Mount*."[2]

10. *Varieties of Religious Experience* by William James was another favorite of early AA (available in paperback). William James was a Harvard professor and founding father of American psychology. This work had a major impact on Bill Wilson and on the development of AA's spiritual principles.[3] The book analyzed "a wide number of religious or conversion experiences." Its objective "was to show that these conversion experiences had validity and value."[4] According to James, whether the experience was a gradual transformation or a lightning experience like Saul on the road to Damascus, it brought the person to "a new state of consciousness" which made possible his or her release from old problems.[5]

ENDNOTES
GLOSSARY
INDEX

CHAPTER TWO
GO TO MEETINGS

1. Archivist, Alcoholics Anonymous World Services, Inc., interview by the author, telephone, 16 June 1994.

2. *The A.A. Group . . . Where It All Begins,* rev. ed. (New York: Alcoholics Anonymous World Services, Inc., 1990), 18–19.

3. *The A.A. Group . . . Where It All Begins,* 19.

4. *Living Sober: Some Methods A.A. Members Have Used for Not Drinking* (New York: Alcoholics Anonymous World Services, Inc., 1975), 82.

CHAPTER FOUR
WORK THE STEPS

1. *Alcoholics Anonymous,* 3d ed. (New York: Alcoholics Anonymous World Services, Inc., 1976), 58.

2. *Twelve Steps and Twelve Traditions* (New York: Alcoholics Anonymous World Services, Inc., 1952), 15.

3. *Voices of Our Co-Founders,* Dr. Bob's last public speech given at AA's first international conference in 1950 (New York: Alcoholics Anonymous World Services, Inc.)

4. *Twelve Steps and Twelve Traditions,* 40.

5. *Twelve Steps and Twelve Traditions,* 26.

6. *Alcoholics Anonymous,* 59.

7. *Alcoholics Anonymous,* 45.

8. *Twelve Steps and Twelve Traditions,* 34–35.

9. *Alcoholics Anonymous,* 83.

CHAPTER FIVE
CALL YOUR SPONSOR

1. *Living Sober: Some Methods A.A. Members Have Used for Not Drinking* (New York: Alcoholics Anonymous World Services, Inc., 1975), 26.

2. *Dr. Bob and the Good Oldtimers: A Biography, with Recollections of Early A.A. in the Midwest* (New York: Alcoholics Anonymous World Services, Inc., 1980), 146.

3. Kurtz, Ernest, *Not-God: A History of Alcoholics Anonymous,* rev. ed. (Center City, Minn.: Hazelden Educational Materials, 1991), 39.

CHAPTER SIX
SAY YOUR PRAYERS

1. *Alcoholics Anonymous,* 3d ed. (New York: Alcoholics Anonymous World Services, Inc., 1976), 45.

2. *'Pass It On,' The Story of Bill Wilson and How the A.A. Message Reached the World* (New York: Alcoholics Anonymous World Services, Inc., 1984), 114.

3. *Alcoholics Anonymous,* 569–70.

4. *Dr. Bob and the Good Oldtimers: A Biography, with Recollections of Early A.A. in the Midwest* (New York: Alcoholics Anonymous World Services, Inc., 1980), 307–8.

5. *Alcoholics Anonymous,* 25.

6. *Alcoholics Anonymous,* 86–87.

7. *Alcoholics Anonymous,* 86.

8. *Alcoholics Anonymous Comes of Age: A Brief History of A.A.* (New York: Alcoholics Anonymous World Services, Inc., 1957), 265.

9. *Alcoholics Anonymous Comes of Age,* 265

10. *Twelve Steps and Twelve Traditions* (New York: Alcoholics Anonymous World Services, Inc., 1952), 102.

11. *Twelve Steps and Twelve Traditions,* 97.

CHAPTER SEVEN
HELP ANOTHER ALCOHOLIC

1. *Alcoholics Anonymous,* 3d ed. (New York: Alcoholics Anonymous World Services, Inc., 1976), 89.

CHAPTER EIGHT
PUT SOBRIETY FIRST

1. *Alcoholics Anonymous,* 3d ed. (New York: Alcoholics Anonymous World Services, Inc., 1976), 143.

2. *Alcoholics Anonymous,* 58.

CHAPTER NINE
TAKE SOBRIETY AND LIFE ONE DAY AT A TIME

1. *'Pass It On,' The Story of Bill Wilson and How the A.A. Message Reached the World* (New York: Alcoholics Anonymous World Services, Inc., 1984), 160–61.

2. Thomsen, Robert, *Bill W.* (New York: Harper and Row, Perennial Library, 1975), 248.

CHAPTER TEN
USE THE SERENITY PRAYER

1. *Alcoholics Anonymous Comes of Age: A Brief History of A.A.* (New York: Alcoholics Anonymous World Services, Inc., 1957), 196.

2. *'Pass It On,' The Story of Bill Wilson and How the A.A. Message Reached the World* (New York: Alcoholics Anonymous World Services, Inc., 1984), 258.

3. Origin of the Serenity Prayer (New York: Alcoholics Anonymous World Services, Inc.).

CHAPTER ELEVEN
REMEMBER: IT'S THE FIRST DRINK THAT GETS US DRUNK
1. American Medical Association, 1964 statement.
2. *Dr. Bob and the Good Oldtimers: A Biography, with Recollections of Early A.A. in the Midwest* (New York: Alcoholics Anonymous World Services, Inc., 1980), 291.

CHAPTER TWELVE
THINK THE DRINK THROUGH
1. *Alcoholics Anonymous,* 3d ed. (New York: Alcoholics Anonymous World Services, Inc., 1976), 285–86.

CHAPTER THIRTEEN
AVOID SLIPPERY PLACES
1. *Alcoholics Anonymous,* 3d ed. (New York: Alcoholics Anonymous World Services, Inc., 1976), 100.
2. *Alcoholics Anonymous,* 101.

CHAPTER FOURTEEN
USE AA SLOGANS
1. Kurtz, Ernest, *Not-God: A History of Alcoholics Anonymous,* rev. ed. (Center City, Minn.: Hazelden Educational Materials, 1991), 321.
2. Kurtz, Ernest, *Not-God,* 42.
3. *Alcoholics Anonymous Comes of Age: A Brief History of A.A.* (New York: Alcoholics Anonymous World Services, Inc., 1957), 214.
4. *Alcoholics Anonymous Comes of Age,* 9.
5. *Twelve Steps and Twelve Traditions* (New York: Alcoholics Anonymous World Services, Inc., 1952), 156.

CHAPTER FIFTEEN
AA GROUPS
1. Archivist, Alcoholics Anonymous World Services, Inc., interview by the author, telephone, 17 June 1994.
2. *Alcoholics Anonymous,* 3d ed. (New York: Alcoholics Anonymous World Services, Inc., 1976), 188–89.
Bill D. was approached by Dr. Bob and Bill Wilson about two days after Dr. Bob's last drink on June 10, 1935. Dr. Bob had said to Bill Wilson, "If you and I are going to stay sober, we had better get busy." Bill D. left the hospital within a

day or two of his first meeting with Bill and Dr. Bob. The date of the founding of the first group would be approximately June 13 or June 14, 1935.

3. *Dr. Bob and the Good Oldtimers: A Biography, with Recollections of Early A.A. in the Midwest* (New York: Alcoholics Anonymous World Services, Inc., 1980), 164.

4. *Dr. Bob and the Good Oldtimers,* 235.

5. Kurtz, Ernest, *Not-God: A History of Alcoholics Anonymous,* rev. ed. (Center City, Minn.: Hazelden Educational Materials, 1991), 77.

6. *Twelve Steps and Twelve Traditions* (New York: Alcoholics Anonymous World Services, Inc., 1952), 139.

7. *The A.A. Group . . . Where It All Begins,* rev. ed. (New York: Alcoholics Anonymous World Services, Inc., 1990), 18.

8. *The AA Group . . . Where It All Begins,* 34–35.

9. *Alcoholics Anonymous,* 77.

CHAPTER SIXTEEN
AA MEETINGS

1. *Alcoholics Anonymous Comes of Age: A Brief History of A.A.* (New York: Alcoholics Anonymous World Services, Inc., 1957), 65–67.

CHAPTER SEVENTEEN
FINDING THE RIGHT MEETING FOR YOU

1. Leerhsen, C., S. D. Lewis, S. Pomper, "Unite and Conquer," *Newsweek* 5 February 1990, 50–55.

2. *Alcoholics Anonymous Comes of Age: A Brief History of A.A.* (New York: Alcoholics Anonymous World Services, Inc., 1957), 109.

3. *Alcoholics Anonymous Comes of Age,* 106.

CHAPTER EIGHTEEN
DUALLY ADDICTED, OR CROSS-ADDICTED, ALCOHOLICS

1. *The A.A. Group . . . Where It All Begins,* rev. ed. (New York: Alcoholics Anonymous World Services, Inc., 1990), 22.

2. *Dr. Bob and the Good Oldtimers: A Biography, with Recollections of Early A.A. in the Midwest* (New York: Alcoholics Anonymous World Services, Inc., 1980), 32.

CHAPTER NINETEEN
DUALLY DIAGNOSED ALCOHOLICS

1. *The A.A. Member—Medications and Other Drugs: A Report from a Group of Physicians in A.A.* (New York: Alcoholics Anonymous World Services, Inc., 1984), 13.

CHAPTER TWENTY-ONE
MEETING CUSTOMS AND ETIQUETTE

1. *Dr. Bob and the Good Oldtimers: A Biography, with Recollections of Early A.A. in the Midwest* (New York: Alcoholics Anonymous World Services, Inc., 1980), 195.

2. *'Pass It On,' The Story of Bill Wilson and How the A.A. Message Reached the World* (New York: Alcoholics Anonymous World Services, Inc., 1984), 219–20.

3. *Dr. Bob and the Good Oldtimers*, 150.

4. Kurtz, Ernest, *Not-God: A History of Alcoholics Anonymous*, rev. ed. (Center City, Minn.: Hazelden Educational Materials, 1991), 279.

5. *Dr. Bob and the Good Oldtimers*, 145–46.

6. *Dr. Bob and the Good Oldtimers*, 146.

7. *Dr. Bob and the Good Oldtimers*, 224.

CHAPTER TWENTY-TWO
ANONYMITY

1. *Alcoholics Anonymous Comes of Age: A Brief History of A.A.* (New York: Alcoholics Anonymous World Services, Inc., 1957), 131–32.

2. *Understanding Anonymity* (New York: Alcoholics Anonymous World Services, Inc., 1981), 6–7.

3. *Understanding Anonymity*, 5.

4. *The A.A. Group . . . Where It All Begins*, rev. ed. (New York: Alcoholics Anonymous World Services, Inc., 1990), 9.

5. *Understanding Anonymity*, 5.

6. *'Pass It On,' The Story of Bill Wilson and How the A.A. Message Reached the World* (New York: Alcoholics Anonymous World Services, Inc., 1984), 311–14.

7. *Alcoholics Anonymous Comes of Age*, 43.

8. *Dr. Bob and the Good Oldtimers: A Biography, with Recollections of Early A.A. in the Midwest* (New York: Alcoholics Anonymous World Services, Inc., 1980), 264.

9. *Dr. Bob and the Good Oldtimers*, 264.

10. *As Bill Sees It: Selected Writings of the A.A.s Co-Founder* (New York: Alcoholics Anonymous World Services, Inc., 1967), 332.

11. *'Pass It On,'* 404.

12. Kurtz, Ernest, *Not-God: A History of Alcoholics Anonymous*, rev. ed. (Center City, Minn.: Hazelden Educational Materials, 1991), 252.

CHAPTER TWENTY-THREE
COMMON QUESTIONS ABOUT ALCOHOL AND AA

1. *The Disease of Alcoholism* (New York: National Council on Alcoholism and Drug Dependence, 1992).

2. *Three Talks to Medical Societies by Bill W., Co-Founder of A.A.* (New York: Alcoholics Anonymous World Services, Inc.), 22.

3. Robertson, Nan, *Getting Better: Inside Alcoholics Anonymous* (New York: Ballantine Books, 1988), 168.

4. Wallace, John, *Writings* (Newport, R. I.: Edgehill Publications, 1989), 306.

5. Volpicelli, T. R., "NaltrExone in the Treatment of Alcohol Dependence," *Archives of General Psychiatry* 49 (November 1992).

6. *Dr. Bob and the Good Oldtimers: A Biography, with Recollections of Early A.A. in the Midwest* (New York: Alcoholics Anonymous World Services, Inc., 1980), 334.

7. *Alcoholics Anonymous Comes of Age: A Brief History of A.A.* (New York: Alcoholics Anonymous World Services, Inc., 1957), 139.

8. *Alcoholics Anonymous Comes of Age,* 139.

9. *'Pass It On,' The Story of Bill Wilson and How the A.A. Message Reached the World* (New York: Alcoholics Anonymous World Services, Inc., 1984), 203.

10. *Alcoholics Anonymous Comes of Age,* 165.

11. *Lois Remembers* (New York: Al-Anon Family Group Headquarters, Inc., 1979), 115.

12. Kurtz, Ernest, *Not-God: A History of Alcoholics Anonymous,* rev. ed. (Center City, Minn.: Hazelden Educational Materials, 1991), 78.

13. Kurtz, Ernest, *Not-God,* 94–96.

14. Kurtz, Ernest, *Not-God,* 94–96.

15. *Twelve Steps and Twelve Traditions* (New York: Alcoholics Anonymous World Services, Inc., 1952), 90.

16. *Alcoholics Anonymous,* 3d ed. (New York: Alcoholics Anonymous World Services, Inc., 1976), xiii.

17. *Alcoholics Anonymous,* 132.

CHAPTER TWENTY-FIVE
YOU CAN HAVE A GOOD TIME SOBER

1. *Alcoholics Anonymous,* 3d ed. (New York: Alcoholics Anonymous World Services, Inc., 1976), 101–2.

2. *Alcoholics Anonymous,* 85.

3. *Dr. Bob and the Good Oldtimers: A Biography, with Recollections of Early A.A. in the Midwest* (New York: Alcoholics Anonymous World Services, Inc., 1980), 148.

4. *Dr. Bob and the Good Oldtimers,* 147.

APPENDIX A
A BRIEF HISTORY OF ALCOHOLICS ANONYMOUS

1. *'Pass It On,' The Story of Bill Wilson and How the A.A. Message Reached the World* (New York: Alcoholics Anonymous World Services, Inc., 1984), 13.

2. *Lois Remembers* (New York: Al-Anon Family Group Headquarters, Inc., 1979), 31.

3. *Dr. Bob and the Good Oldtimers: A Biography, with Recollections of Early A.A. in the Midwest* (New York: Alcoholics Anonymous World Services, Inc., 1980), 33, 125.

4. Robertson, Nan, *Getting Better: Inside Alcoholics Anonymous* (New York: Ballantine Books, Fawcett Crest Books 1988), 24.

5. Kurtz, Ernest, *Not-God: A History of Alcoholics Anonymous,* rev. 2d ed. (Center City, Minn.: Hazelden Educational Materials, 1991).

6. *'Pass It On,'* 100-1.

7. *'Pass It On,'* 111.

8. *'Pass It On,'* 111.

9. *'Pass It On,'* 116–18.

10. *'Pass It On,'* 118–120.

11. *'Pass It On,'* 127.

12. B., Mel, *New Wine: The Spiritual Roots of the Twelve Step Miracle* (Center City, Minn.: Hazelden Educational Materials, 1991), 30.

13. *Alcoholics Anonymous Comes of Age: A Brief History of A.A.* (New York: Alcoholics Anonymous World Services, Inc., 1957), 39.

14. *'Pass It On,'* 133.

15. Thomsen, Robert, *Bill W.* (New York: Harper and Row, Perennial Library, 1975), 233.

16. *'Pass It On,'* 135.

17. Thomsen, Robert, *Bill W.,* 235–36.

18. *Dr. Bob and the Good Oldtimers,* 66.

19. *Dr. Bob and the Good Oldtimers,* 66.

20. *Dr. Bob and the Good Oldtimers,* 70.

21. *Dr. Bob and the Good Oldtimers,* 156–70.

APPENDIX B
THE BIG BOOK

1. Thomsen, Robert, *Bill W.* (New York: Harper and Row, Perennial Library, 1975), 266.

2. Thomsen, Robert, *Bill W.,* 268.

3. *'Pass It On,' The Story of Bill Wilson and How the A.A. Message Reached the World* (New York: Alcoholics Anonymous World Services, Inc., 1984), 193.

4. Thomsen, Robert, *Bill W.,* 277–78.

5. *Lois Remembers* (New York: Al-Anon Family Group Headquarters, Inc., 1979), 113.

6. Thomsen, Robert, *Bill W.,* 282.

7. *Alcoholics Anonymous Comes of Age: A Brief History of A.A.* (New York: Alcoholics Anonymous World Services, Inc., 1957), 161.

8. *Alcoholics Anonymous Comes of Age,* 162–63.

9. *Alcoholics Anonymous Comes of Age,* 167.

10. Thomsen, Robert, *Bill W.,* 284.

11. *'Pass It On,'* 200.

12. Kurtz, Ernest, *Not-God: A History of Alcoholics Anonymous,* rev. ed. (Center City, Minn.: Hazelden Educational Materials, 1991), 74

13. *Lois Remembers,* 114; *Alcoholics Anonymous Comes of Age,* 165–66.

14. *'Pass It On,'* 202.

15. *'Pass It On,'* 203.

16. Kurtz, Ernest, *Not-God,* 92.

17. Archivist, Alcoholics Anonymous World Services, Inc., interview by the author, telephone, 5 July 1995.

18. *Lois Remembers,* 115.

19. *Lois Remembers,* 115.

20. *'Pass It On,'* 205.

21. *Alcoholics Anonymous,* 3d ed. (New York: Alcoholics Anonymous World Services, Inc., 1976), xi.

22. *'Pass It On,'* 356–57.

23. *Alcoholics Anonymous,* xi.

24. Archivist, Alcoholics Anonymous World Services, Inc., interview by the author, telephone, 17 June 1994.

APPENDIX C
OFTEN QUOTED PASSAGES

1. Kurtz, Ernest, *Not-God: A History of Alcoholics Anonymous,* rev. ed. (Center City, Minn.: Hazelden Educational Materials, 1991), 254.

2. B., Mel, *New Wine: The Spiritual Roots of the Twelve Step Miracle* (Center City, Minn.: Hazelden Educational Materials, 1991), 78.

3. *'Pass It On,' The Story of Bill Wilson and How the A.A. Message Reached the World* (New York: Alcoholics Anonymous World Services, Inc., 1984), 120–21.

4. Thomsen, Robert, *Bill W.* (New York: Harper and Row, Perennial Library, 1975), 337.

5. *'Pass It On,'* 258.

6. *Alcoholics Anonymous Comes of Age: A Brief History of A.A.* (New York: Alcoholics Anonymous World Services, Inc., 1957), 204.

7. *Alcoholics Anonymous Comes of Age,* 288.

APPENDIX D

OTHER BOOKS ABOUT AA

1. B., Mel, *New Wine: The Spiritual Roots of the Twelve Step Miracle* (Center City, Minn.: Hazelden Educational Materials, 1991), 5.

2. *Dr. Bob and the Good Oldtimers: A Biography, with Recollections of Early A.A. in the Midwest* (New York: Alcoholics Anonymous World Services, Inc., 1980), 151.

3. *'Pass It On,' The Story of Bill Wilson and How the A.A. Message Reached the World* (New York: Alcoholics Anonymous World Services, Inc., 1984), 124–25.

4. *'Pass It On,'* 124.

5. *'Pass It On,'* 125.

Glossary
Of Common AA Words
And Phrases

This glossary is a handy tool for finding the meaning of unfamiliar words or phrases that you hear in AA meetings. In some cases, the source or original use of the term is explained. If the word or phrase appears in one of the chapters of this book, you are referred to that chapter for further information. If the phrase is related to another entry in the glossary, you are directed to it.

A

AA Clubs: Meeting facilities that are available for the exclusive use of AA groups. Meetings at AA clubs are open to all AA members. See "AA Clubs" in chapter 15, "AA Groups," for more information.

AA General Service Board (the Trustees): A board composed of fourteen AA trustees and seven nonalcoholic trustees that serves to safeguard AA's traditions and funds. It has the legal responsibility of overseeing AA's three operating service units: General Service Office (GSO), AA World Services, Inc., and The AA Grapevine, Inc.[1]*

AA General Service Conference: A conference that links the AA groups to the General Service Office and Board. It is the group conscience for AA as a whole. The conference meets for six days each year, but the 135 conference members are active in conference affairs throughout the year. Conference members are elected as representatives from each of ninety-one area assemblies which are themselves elected by General Service Representatives from all AA groups.

---

*Endnotes for the Glossary appear on pages 202–4.

AA General Service Office (GSO): The storehouse of AA's shared knowledge and experience. It helps AA fulfill its primary purpose by
- Providing service, information, and AA experience to groups worldwide.
- Publishing and distributing AA books and pamphlets.
- Supporting the activities of the General Service Board.
- Carrying forward recommendations of the General Service Conference.
- Dealing with the general public.

AA General Service Representative (GSR): A person who serves as an individual group's link to the General Service Conference. Sometimes called "the guardians of the Traditions," GSRs are elected from each AA group to serve on area committees. Delegates from these area committees are then elected to serve as members of the General Service Conference.

A.A. Grapevine: The pocket-sized monthly publication for AA members available by subscription. "The Grapevine," as it is usually called, consists of a monthly calendar of AA events, regular features, and special articles on issues and topics of interest to AA members. It is sometimes called "our meeting in print."

AA Group: Any two or three alcoholics gathered together for sobriety provided that, as a group, they have no other affiliation. See chapter 15, "AA Groups," for more information.

AA Preamble: A statement that briefly explains AA and its purpose. The Preamble is read at the beginning of most AA meetings. It is based on a portion of the foreword to the first edition of the Big Book. See "AA Preamble" in appendix C, "Often Quoted Passages," for the complete text.

AA Promises: See "Twelve Promises."

AA World Services, Inc.: "AA World Services, Inc. is a nonprofit corporation which manages the AA General Service Office, publishes all AA literature and serves groups in foreign countries that do not have national headquarters of their own."[2]

AA's Primary Purpose: According to the AA Preamble, "Our primary purpose is to stay sober and help other alcoholics to achieve sobriety."

A Vision for You: The title of chapter 11 of the Big Book. This phrase is often used to refer to the last three paragraphs of chapter 11 and is sometimes read at AA meetings. See "A Vision for You" in appendix C, "Often Quoted Passages," for the complete text.

ABCs: Three basic ideas for AAs to understand: "(a) That we were alcoholic and could not manage our own lives, (b) That probably no human power could have relieved our alcoholism, (c) That God could and would if He were sought."[3]

Abstinence: Not having any alcohol to drink, period. Abstinence is the only treatment for the disease of alcoholism. In AA, abstinence is maintained one day at a time.

Acceptance: One of AA's great themes summarized in the Serenity Prayer. As AA members, we strive to accept the things in life we cannot change, including our alcoholism and the fact that we cannot drink normally. For the most part, all that we can change is ourselves. See also "Serenity Prayer."

Action: See "Into Action."

Al-Anon Family Groups: A Twelve Step fellowship for family members and friends of alcoholics. It was cofounded by Lois Wilson, the wife of AA's cofounder Bill Wilson. Al-Anon uses exactly the same Twelve Steps as AA, but is entirely separate from AA. The name Al-Anon was created from Alcoholics Anonymous by combining the first syllables of each word. See also "Alateen."

Alateen: A Twelve Step fellowship for teenagers with alcoholism in their families. Founded in 1957, Alateen is part of Al-Anon and uses the same Twelve Steps as AA. See also "Al-Anon Family Groups."

Alcoholic Grandiosity: The phrase refers to an alcoholic's insistence on having his or her own way regardless of the will of the Higher Power or the demands of reality. It is self-will run riot. See also "Self-Centeredness" and "Self-Will Run Riot."

Alcoholic Insanity: An untrue belief held by some alcoholics that they can control their drinking or that they can somehow drink normally again.

Alcoholism: An AA pamphlet defines alcoholism in this way, "While there is no formal 'AA definition' of alcoholism, most of us agree that, for us, it could be described *as a physical compulsion, coupled with a mental obsession.* We mean that we had a distinct physical desire to consume alcohol beyond our capacity to control it, and in defiance of all rules of common sense. We not only had an abnormal craving for alcohol, but we frequently yielded to it at the worst possible times. We did not know when (or how) to stop drinking."[4]

The American Medical Association formally recognized alcoholism as a disease in 1972. In 1956, it had classified alcoholism as a "treatable illness." Alcoholism results from a genetic predisposition working in combination with psychological and environmental factors. There is no cure. Abstinence is the only treatment. See chapter 23, "Common Questions about Alcohol and AA," for a formal definition of alcoholism.

Alcoholism as a Progressive Disease: The term "progressive" is used to describe alcoholism because, as a rule, it only gets worse if it is left untreated. Abstinence is the only treatment.

Alcoholism as a Threefold Illness: The Big Book describes alcoholism as a threefold illness that affects its victims physically, mentally, and spiritually.

The Big Book states, "When the spiritual malady is overcome, we straighten out mentally and physically."[5]

Alcoholism Cure: There is no cure for alcoholism. But it can be treated, one day at a time, through abstinence made possible by membership in AA.

Amends: Repairing the damage that our past behavior has caused. Making amends is an important part of Twelve Step recovery. In accordance with AA's Eighth Step, we make amends for past behavior that has harmed others. In accordance with the Tenth Step, we promptly admit it when we are wrong and make amends. See "Steps Four through Ten," in chapter 4, "Work the Steps," for a more detailed discussion of amends.

An Easier, Softer Way: The attempt by some AA members to find an easier, softer way to recover from alcoholism than having to work the Twelve Steps. The phrase is taken from chapter 5 of the Big Book, "We thought we could find an easier, softer way. But we could not."[6]

Anger: See "Justifiable Anger."

Anniversary: The annual anniversary of the date on which an AA member stopped drinking. The term "anniversary" is generally used in the East and Midwest, and the term "birthday" is used in the West and Southwest to mean the same.

Anonymity: The AA concept of anonymity is captured in this saying, "Who you see here, what you hear here, when you leave here, let it stay here." Anonymity is so important to AA that the word "Anonymous" is part of its name. To break anonymity is to reveal one's own membership or someone else's membership in AA or to repeat something that was said by someone in an AA meeting. Refer to chapter 22, "Anonymity," for a fuller explanation of this major AA tradition.

Antabuse: An oral prescription drug that makes a person deathly ill if he or she drinks alcohol. Antabuse is used by some alcoholics as an aid in not drinking. Antabuse is the brand name for disulfiram.

Any Length: The phrase refers to an AA member's willingness to "go to any length" to stay sober. It means being willing to do whatever is necessary to maintain sobriety and captures the idea of always putting sobriety first. The phrase is taken from chapter 5 of the Big Book, "If you have decided you want what we have and are willing to go to any length to get it—then you are ready to take certain steps." The same idea appears in a less famous sentence in the Big Book: "Remember it was agreed at the beginning *we would go to any lengths for victory over alcohol.*"[7]

B

Babies: See "Pigeon."

Balance: The term refers to the AA goal of achieving emotional balance as a result of working the Twelve Steps.

Big Book: The nickname given to the basic text of Alcoholics Anonymous which is formally entitled *Alcoholics Anonymous*. See appendix B, "The Big Book," for more information on the Big Book and its history.

Big Book Study Meeting: An AA meeting devoted to the study of the Big Book.

Bill Wilson: See "Wilson, Bill."

Birthday: The annual anniversary of the date on which an AA member got sober. The term "birthday" is generally used in the West and Southwest and the term "anniversary" is used in the East and Midwest to mean the same.

Blackout: A period of amnesia extending from a few minutes to a few hours or even days as a result of heavy alcohol use. While in a blackout, the person continues to function and may drive a car, engage in conversation, take a trip, and so on—but he or she will have no memory of it later.

Bondage of Self: Alcoholic self-centeredness and self-will. The phrase is taken from the Third Step Prayer in chapter five of the Big Book, "Relieve me of the bondage of self, that I may better do Thy will."[8]

Box 4-5-9: The AA General Service Office's newsletter which is GSO's primary tool for communicating with the Fellowship.

Breaking Anonymity: To reveal one's own membership or someone else's membership in AA or to repeat something that was said by someone in an AA meeting. See chapter 22, "Anonymity," for a full explanation of when it is appropriate and inappropriate to break anonymity.

C

Cafeteria Style: Newcomers are sometimes advised that AA meetings are like cafeterias: you can take what you like and leave the rest. Within reason, that advice is true. But we have to be careful not to leave something we ought to be taking. Especially in the early days of sobriety, we need to hear some things we may not want to hear. It's easy enough to reject the truth because we don't like it. We can approach AA meetings with a "cafeteria" in mind as long as we have an *open* mind and are willing to listen. We need to remember that if our judgment had been so great in the first place, we wouldn't be in the shape we're in that brought us to AA.

Came to Believe: This phrase is taken from AA's Second Step, "Came to believe that a Power greater than ourselves could restore us to sanity." It is sometimes broken down in this way: First, we *came* physically to AA. Then we *came to* our senses, out of our denial and our alcoholic fantasies. Finally, we *came to believe* that a Power greater than ourselves could restore us to sanity.

Care of God: The phrase is taken from AA's Third Step in which we "made a decision to turn our will and our lives over to the care of God *as we understood Him.*" The Twelve and Twelve states, "the effectiveness of the whole A.A. program will rest upon how well and earnestly we have tried to come to 'a decision to turn our will and our lives over to the care of God *as we understood Him.*'"[9]

Carry the Message: To take the good news to the alcoholic who still suffers that recovery from the disease of alcoholism is possible through Alcoholics Anonymous. It is the responsibility of each AA member to carry the message of recovery to the alcoholic who still suffers. Helping another alcoholic is one of the primary ways in which we stay sober.

The expression "carry the message" is taken from AA's Twelfth Step, "Having had a spiritual awakening as the result of these steps, we tried to carry this message to alcoholics, and to practice these principles in all our affairs." It is also contained in AA's Fifth Tradition, "Each group has but one primary purpose—to carry its message to the alcoholic who still suffers."

Carry the Message, Not the Alcoholic: It is our responsibility as members of Alcoholics Anonymous to be willing to carry the message of AA recovery to the alcoholic who still suffers. But it is not our responsibility to get that alcoholic sober. Only the alcoholic himself or herself can make that decision. Only the alcoholic can take the actions necessary to achieve sobriety.

Cash Register Honesty: A technical kind of honesty that means we don't steal. It is often compared to another, deeper kind of self-honesty and honesty-with-others about who we are that is also necessary for recovery.

Central Office: A local coordinating office for AA groups. It also acts as a point of contact for the general public and as a clearinghouse for information on AA meetings and activities. In some cities, it is called Intergroup.

Chapter Five: The reference is to chapter 5, "How It Works," of the Big Book. Chapter 5 explains how AA works as a program of recovery. It lists the Twelve Steps and discusses in detail the first four Steps. The chapter begins, "Rarely have we seen a person fail who has thoroughly followed our path."[10] A portion of the chapter is sometimes read after the preamble at the beginning of AA meetings.

Character Defects: The defects of character that we identify in our Fourth Step inventory and which we try to eliminate as part of our recovery program. In the "searching and fearless moral inventory" that we conduct in the Fourth Step, we identify a list of character defects in ourselves. In the Fifth Step, we admit these defects to God, to ourselves, and to another human being. In the Sixth through Tenth Steps, we try to eliminate these defects with God's help and to make amends for the things we have done wrong.

Chip System: The custom followed by some AA groups of handing out small medallions called "chips" to mark various anniversaries of AA members' sobriety dates. Many AA members, especially newcomers, carry a chip with them as a reminder of their commitment to sobriety. See "Chip System" in chapter 21, "Meeting Customs and Etiquette," for more information.

Chips: See "Chip System."

Civilian: AA slang for someone who is not a member of AA.

Closed Meeting: An AA meeting that is "closed" to nonalcoholics. Only alcoholics and those who think they may have a problem with alcohol are allowed to attend. See "Types of Meetings" in chapter 16, "AA Meetings," for more information.

Clubs: See "AA Clubs."

Commitments: The word refers to service work within an AA group that an AA member has agreed to perform for a specified period of time. For example, to serve as group secretary. The term is especially popular in California.

Conference-Approved Literature: Literature that has been approved for publication by the AA General Service Conference. Since AA "neither endorses nor opposes any causes" and "has no opinion on outsides issues," all official AA literature must adhere to these strict guidelines. Conference-approved literature means that the information it contains is in line with AA positions (on internal issues) and traditions.

Confidentiality: Whatever is said in an AA meeting is confidential and should not be repeated outside that meeting.

Conscious Contact: Staying in regular touch with our Higher Power through prayer and meditation. Maintaining conscious contact with a Power greater than ourselves is a key element in AA recovery. Prayer and meditation are "our principal means of conscious contact with God."[11] The phrase is taken from AA's Eleventh Step, "Sought through prayer and meditation to improve our conscious contact with God *as we understood Him,* praying only for knowledge of His will for us and the power to carry that out."

Constitutionally Incapable of Being Honest: Not capable of being honest. The ability to be honest with oneself is essential to recovery. Anyone who is constitutionally incapable of being honest has a less-than-average chance of recovering. The phrase is taken from chapter 5 of the Big Book. The context is this: "Those who do not recover are people who cannot or will not completely give themselves to this simple program, usually men and women who are constitutionally incapable of being honest with themselves. There are such unfortunates. They are not at fault; they seem to have been born that way. They are naturally incapable of grasping and developing a manner of living which demands rigorous honesty. Their chances are less than average."[12]

Contempt Prior to Investigation: A warning against being closed to new ideas.

Open-mindedness is a necessary part of recovery. The phrase appears in a quotation of Herbert Spencer's contained in appendix 2 of the Big Book, "There is a principle which is a bar against all information, which is proof against all arguments and which cannot fail to keep a man in everlasting ignorance—that principle is contempt prior to investigation."[13] See also "Open-Mindedness."

Controlled Drinking: The phrase refers to a person's decision to restrict the number of drinks he or she has to some predetermined limit. It is sometimes used in reference to alcoholics, but it does not apply to them. Alcoholics cannot control their drinking problem by limiting the number of drinks they have as an alternative to complete abstinence. The Big Book states, "We alcoholics are men and women who have lost the ability to control our drinking. We know that no real alcoholic *ever* recovers control."[14] "The idea that somehow, someday, he will control and enjoy his drinking is the great obsession of every abnormal drinker. The persistence of this illusion is astonishing. Many pursue it into the gates of insanity or death."[15] See "What about Controlled Drinking?" in chapter 23, "Common Questions about Alcohol and AA," for more detailed information on this topic.

Courage to Change: Recovery is all about change, and change is all about courage. That's why those in recovery pray for "the courage to change." Courage is not the *absence* of fear, but the overcoming of it. Fear is a natural part of the disease of addiction; *overcoming* it is a natural part of recovery. The expression is taken from the Serenity Prayer: "God, grant me the serenity to accept the things I cannot change, the courage to change the things I can, and the wisdom to know the difference."

Cross-Addiction: Being dependent upon two drugs (for example, alcohol and cocaine). Dr. Bob, AA's cofounder, was cross-addicted to alcohol and sedatives. The term "dual addiction" has the same meaning.

Cross-Talk: When one AA member directly addresses another member during the sharing part of an AA meeting and offers advice. In AA, we are expected to share our experience, strength, and hope with one another rather than offer advice or instruction. Therefore, it is against AA customs to engage in cross-talk during an AA meeting. Refer to "Cross-Talk" in chapter 21, "Meeting Customs and Etiquette," for more information.

Cunning, Baffling, Powerful!: The expression refers to (a) alcohol for the alcoholic and (b) the disease of alcoholism. It comes from the following sentence in chapter 5 of the Big Book, "Remember that we deal with alcohol—cunning, baffling, powerful! Without help it is too much for us."[16]

D

Daily Inventory: Step Ten calls for a daily personal inventory. It is the same kind of searching and fearless moral inventory that we took in Step Four except that it deals with the past twenty-four hours. Our goal is to reduce the damage our character defects cause and to keep our relationship with ourselves and others on an even keel.

Daily Reprieve: The word "reprieve" means "temporary relief from." We have a daily reprieve from our alcoholism that is dependent upon the maintenance of our spiritual condition. The phrase appears in chapter 6 of the Big Book, "We are not cured of alcoholism. What we really have is a daily reprieve contingent on the maintenance of our spiritual condition."[17]

Defects of Character: See "Character Defects."

Denial: A person's refusal to admit that he or she is an alcoholic; denial is a symptom of the disease of alcoholism. It is this symptom that makes recovery so difficult, because denial must be overcome for recovery to take place. Denial is never completely overcome, however, and must be guarded against during recovery. The humorous AA saying that relates to this issue is "Denial is not a river in Egypt."

Design for Living: The phrase refers to the AA program of recovery and to the new life that it offers alcoholics. The words appear in chapter 2 of the Big Book, as follows: "A new life has been given us or, if you prefer, 'a design for living' that really works."[18]

Desire Chip: A medallion given out at AA meetings to anyone who has "a desire to stop drinking." In some meetings it is also referred to as a "twenty-four-hour chip." See also "Chip System." Refer to "Chip System" in chapter 21, "Meeting Customs and Etiquette," for more information.

Detox: Slang for "detoxification," the process by which an alcoholic withdraws from the use of alcohol.

Discussion Meeting: An AA meeting in which the leader shares his or her experience, strength, and hope for a few minutes and then suggests a topic for discussion.

Double Winner: An AA member who is also a member of Al-Anon.

Dr. Bob: The nickname used in AA for Dr. Robert Smith, AA's cofounder. See also "Smith, Robert Holbrook, M.D."

Drinking Dream: A recovering alcoholic's sleeping dream in which he or she drinks again. No one knows exactly what a drinking dream means, but it can be very disturbing to the alcoholic in recovery. See "What Does It Mean If I Have a Drinking Dream?" in chapter 23, "Common Questions about Alcohol and AA," for more information.

Drunk-a-logue: That portion of an AA member's story that deals with the drinking period of his or her life.

Dry: Being abstinent from alcohol. Sobriety as practiced within AA is more than just abstinence, however. It is a way of life based on spiritual principles. Being dry, of course, is the basis of everything else, but true sobriety is more. To remain dry without changing intellectually, emotionally, or spiritually is to run a serious risk of drinking again and to experience unhappiness and dissatisfaction. The Big Book says, "We feel that elimination of our drinking is but a beginning."[19]

Dry Bender: A phrase used in the Big Book to mean a dry drunk. See "Dry Drunk."

Dry Drunk: A condition characterized by a return to alcoholic thinking and behavior even though the alcoholic has not yet returned to drinking. One of the best ways out of a "dry drunk" is to work with another still-suffering alcoholic. See "What Is a 'Dry Drunk'?" in chapter 23, "Common Questions about Alcohol and AA," for more information.

Dual Addiction: See "Cross-Addiction."

Dual Diagnosis: An AA member who has an emotional or psychiatric disorder in addition to alcoholism. The other diagnosis may be major depression, manic-depression (bipolar disorder), personality disorder, panic disorder, and so on. Bill Wilson, AA's cofounder, was dually diagnosed with depression.

E

Earthling: AA slang for someone who is not an AA member.

Earth People: AA slang for people who are not members of AA.

Easing God Out (E.G.O.): This acronym is a reminder that it is God's will for us rather than our self-will that guides our life in sobriety. When self-will and self-centeredness return, we have abandoned the decision we made in the Third Step. Instead of "turning it over," we are "taking it back." We have eased God out of our lives.

Enabling: A term used to describe "loving" behavior that works against a drinking alcoholic's recovery because it keeps him or her from having to be responsible for the consequences of his or her behavior. Examples of enabling are telling the boss that the alcoholic is sick with the flu when he or she is hung over, or cleaning up the vomit from the night before. In both cases, the alcoholic should have to face the consequences of his or her drinking by having to do those chores himself or herself.

Ex-Alcoholic: There is no such thing as an ex-alcoholic since there is no cure for the disease of alcoholism. Even alcoholics in recovery remain alcoholics. They are simply nondrinking alcoholics.

Experience, Strength, and Hope: When we share in AA about our recovery from alcoholism, we are expected to share our experience, strength, and hope. We do not offer advice, instruction, or therapy. The phrase appears in the AA Preamble, as follows: "Alcoholics Anonymous is a fellowship of men and women who share their experience, strength and hope with each other that they may solve their common problem and help others to recover from alcoholism."

F

Faith without Works is Dead: A biblical expression used in the Fellowship to mean that AA is a program of action. It appears in chapter 6 of the Big Book in this context, "Now we need more action, without which we find that 'Faith without works is dead.'"[20] It was the favorite biblical quotation of Anne Smith, Dr. Bob's wife.

Fellowship, the: A nickname used by AA members to refer to Alcoholics Anonymous. Use of the term appears in several places in the Big Book, including the foreword to the first edition and chapter 7, "Working with Others: "On your first visit [to a newcomer] tell him about the Fellowship of Alcoholics Anonymous."[21]

Forgiveness: The act of giving up feelings of resentment toward someone. Forgiveness of those who have harmed us is an essential part of Step Five. See "Steps Four through Ten" in chapter 4, "Work the Steps," for a more detailed discussion of the term.

Fourth Step Inventory: The "searching and fearless moral inventory" suggested by AA's Fourth Step. See also "Character Defects." Refer to "Steps Four through Ten" in chapter 4, "Work the Steps," for more information.

G

Geographical: See "Geographical Cure."

Geographical Cure: An effort to cure our alcoholism by moving to a new city and "starting over" while still drinking. It doesn't work.

God as We Understand Him: See "Higher Power."

God of Our Understanding: See "Higher Power."

God's Time: The expression reminds us that the events of the world unfold according to God's time, not our own. When we grow impatient because the things we want are not happening fast enough to suit us, we try to remember that it is not up to us to set the timetable for God's events. It is up to God.

Grandiosity: See "Alcoholic Grandiosity."

Grapevine: See *"A.A. Grapevine."*

Gratitude List: A written list of all the things for which we are grateful. When we are feeling scared, depressed, or self-pitying, it is suggested that we make a gratitude list; it is an effective way to counteract depression and self-pity.

Group Conscience: The mechanism through which an AA group makes decisions about matters affecting the group as a whole. The group conscience is expressed through a meeting held for that purpose immediately before or after a regular AA meeting. Every member of the group is entitled to vote, and everyone is a member who so declares himself or herself.

Gut-Level Honesty: See "Rigorous Honesty."

H

Half Measures: The phrase is taken from chapter 5 of the Big Book, "Half measures availed us nothing. We stood at the turning point."[22] It is a reminder that an "easier, softer way" that tries to short-cut the Twelve Steps won't bring us the quality of recovery we seek. The phrase also reminds us to put our sobriety first.

H.A.L.T.: An acronym that stands for Hungry, Angry, Lonely, or Tired. This simple acronym reminds us to avoid these states in order to protect our recovery. See "H.A.L.T." in chapter 14, "Use AA Slogans," for more information.

Happy, Joyous, and Free: To be happy, joyous, and free is one of the goals—and rewards—of our recovery from alcoholism. The quotation is taken from chapter 9 of the Big Book, "We are sure God wants us to be happy, joyous, and free. We cannot subscribe to the belief that this life is a vale of tears, though it once was just that for many of us."[23]

High Bottom Drunk: An alcoholic entering AA who has retained most or all of the following: family, home, job, car, physical health, reputation, and so on. Everyone entering AA has hit some kind of emotional bottom, but for some the social, legal, or financial bottom may be relatively high. The more one has managed to retain upon entering AA, the higher his or her bottom is said to be. See also "Hitting Bottom."

Higher Power: A self-defined Power greater than ourselves to which we turn for assistance and guidance in our sober lives. In our drinking days, alcohol was the power greater than ourselves to which we turned over our will and our lives. In sobriety, we choose a different kind of Power for that purpose. Since AA is a spiritual program rather than a religious one, the definition of that "Higher Power" is left entirely to the individual AA member.

Hitting Bottom: Reaching such a state of hopelessness that we become willing to admit complete defeat in dealing with our alcoholism, and we become willing to do whatever is necessary to achieve sobriety. The "bottom" we hit at the end of our drinking days is primarily emotional and spiritual. But it may also be physical, financial, social, and legal. "Why all this insistence that every

A.A. must hit bottom first?" asks the Twelve and Twelve. "The answer is that few people will sincerely try to practice the A.A. program unless they have hit bottom."[24] Bill Wilson wrote, "You must always remember that 'hitting bottom' is the essence of getting hold of A.A.—really."[25] See also "Intervention."

Home Group: The group that an AA member attends on a regular basis and calls "home." Most AA members have a home group. The members of our home group are like the members of an extended family who have come to know us well in our sobriety. Our home group is our strongest link to the AA Fellowship.

Homer: A housebound or handicapped AA member. Since homers cannot attend meetings (or only a few), they rely on the Big Book, telephone calls, and written correspondence to stay sober. Homers often communicate directly with AA's General Service Office in New York City.

Honesty: See "Cash Register Honesty," "Rigorous Honesty," and "Constitutionally Incapable of Being Honest."

H.O.W.: This acronym stands for Honesty, Open-Mindedness, and Willingness—the keys to recovery. Without openness, we won't listen to the principles of recovery offered to us. Without willingness, we won't act on what we hear. And without honesty, we won't see the problems that have to be faced and solved for recovery to take place. The three components of the acronym are listed in this sentence in appendix 2 of the Big Book, "Willingness, honesty and open mindedness are the essentials of recovery. But these are indispensable."[26]

H.O.W. It Works: The acronym H.O.W. stands for honesty, open-mindedness, and willingness. The expression is a play on the title of chapter 5, "How it Works," of the Big Book. Chapter 5 explains the AA program of recovery and lists the Twelve Steps.

Humility: The Twelve and Twelve says that humility is "the main key to sobriety."[27] And that the "basic ingredient of all humility [is] a desire to seek and do God's will."[28] "Perfect humility," Bill Wilson wrote, "would be a full willingness, in all times and places, to find and to do the will of God."[29] "The attainment of greater humility is the foundation principle of each of A.A.'s Twelve Steps. For without some degree of humility, no alcoholic can stay sober at all. Nearly all A.A.'s have found, too, that unless they develop much more of this precious quality than may be required just for sobriety, they still haven't much chance of becoming truly happy."[30]

I

I Am Responsible: The expression is shorthand for the responsibility that each AA member has to help any alcoholic who asks for help. It is taken from the

Responsibility Declaration adopted at AA's 1965 International Convention. The Declaration reads, "I am responsible. When anyone, anywhere, reaches out for help, I want the hand of A.A. always to be there. And for that: I am responsible."[31]

Identification: As we listen in AA meetings, we try to identify with the speaker. Identification is one of the ways in which we overcome the denial associated with our alcoholism. When an alcoholic in recovery honestly tells his or her story, openly admitting personal weaknesses and vulnerability, we can identify with him or her, and our denial is momentarily overcome.[32] This discovery formed one of the fundamental principles of AA: that one alcoholic could help another alcoholic stay sober. See also "Denial."

Insanity: The term is usually defined within AA as doing the same thing but expecting different results. It relates to AA's Second Step, "Came to believe that a Power greater than ourselves could restore us to sanity."

Intergroup: A local coordinating office for AA groups. It also acts as a point of contact for the general public and as a clearinghouse for information on AA meetings and activities. In some cities, it is called the Central Office.

Internationalist: A seagoing AA member who finds himself or herself without a meeting for long periods of time. Internationalists rely on the Big Book, telephone calls, and written correspondence to stay sober and often communicate directly with AA's General Service Office in New York City.

Intervention: The process by which family members and friends of an alcoholic confront the alcoholic about his or her behavior and the negative effects of that behavior on them. The goal of an intervention is to break through the alcoholic's denial system and motivate him or her to enter recovery. Intervention often makes it possible to interrupt the addiction process before an individual hits his or her "natural" bottom.

Into Action: AA is a program of action. Good intentions, intellectualizing, and theorizing aid the disease and not our recovery from it if they are divorced from action. The expression comes from the title of chapter 6 of the Big Book, "Into Action." At AA's twentieth anniversary convention, Bill Wilson said, "A.A. is more than a set of principles; it is a society of recovered alcoholics in action."[33]

J

Justifiable Anger: Anger that we feel justified in holding on to because of the events that caused it. According to the Big Book, there is no justification for remaining angry about anything. Often we "justify" the anger so we don't have to look at ourselves and our own part in creating it. The Twelve and Twelve reminds us, "It is a spiritual axiom that every time we are disturbed, no matter what the cause, there is something wrong *with us.* If somebody hurts us and we are sore, we are in the wrong also. But are there no exceptions to this rule? What about 'justifiable' anger? If somebody cheats us, aren't we entitled to be mad? Can't we be properly angry with self-righteous folk? For us of A.A. these are dangerous exceptions. We have found that justified anger ought to be left to those better qualified to handle it."[34] Anger is to be felt and then released, not harbored and turned into a resentment.

L

Lack of Power: As alcoholics, our central problem is powerlessness over alcohol. The phrase comes from chapter 4 of the Big Book, "Lack of power, that was our dilemma. We had to find a power by which we could live, and it had to be a *Power greater than ourselves.*"[35] Use of the word "dilemma" reminds us that we face a remarkable paradox in recovery. In order to overcome alcoholism, we must first admit that we are powerless over it. If we admit to that powerlessness, we are given the power we need. If we insist that we are not powerless, that power is denied to us. See also "Surrender."

Lead: The term "lead" is used in some parts of the United States to mean a leader's opening remarks in an AA meeting. It usually lasts five to ten minutes and introduces the discussion topic.

Legacies: See "Three Legacies of AA."

Low Bottom Drunk: An alcoholic entering AA who has lost most or all of the following: family, home, job, car, physical health, reputation, and so on. Everyone entering AA has hit some kind of emotional bottom, but for some the social, legal, or financial bottom may be especially low. The more one has lost upon entering AA, the lower his or her bottom is said to be. See also "Hitting Bottom."

M

Maximum Service: The phrase comes from chapter 6 of the Big Book, "Our real purpose is to fit ourselves to be of maximum service to God and the people about us."[36]

Meeting in Print: AA's monthly publication, the *A.A. Grapevine,* is often called "our meeting in print."

Meetings: At the heart of Twelve Step recovery are the meetings. It is here that the members share their experience, strength, and hope with one another and find recovery. See chapter 16, "AA Meetings," and chapter 17, "Finding the Right Meeting for You," for more information.

N

NaltrExone: A prescription drug that reduces the physical craving for alcohol in some alcoholics when combined with a regular counseling program including membership in AA. It is marketed under the trade name ReVia and was approved by the FDA in 1995.

Ninety in Ninety: The expression refers to the suggestion made to newcomers that they attend one AA meeting a day for the first ninety days of their sobriety. See chapter 2, "Go to Meetings," for a more detailed discussion.

O

Old-Timer: An AA member who has been continuously sober for a significant period of time. The definition of "significant" is open to interpretation. As a general rule, an old-timer is someone who has been sober ten or more years.

One Day at a Time: This expression describes one of AA's basic strategies for staying sober. It means to stay in recovery by choosing not to drink for the one day in which we find ourselves. That specific twenty-four hours is the only time period about which we are concerned. We can take life and sobriety one hour at a time or one minute at a time if we need to in order to stay sober. Refer to chapter 9, "Take Sobriety and Life One Day at a Time," for more information.

Open Meeting: An AA meeting that anyone who is interested in Alcoholics Anonymous may attend. An open meeting is to be compared to a closed meeting, which is restricted to alcoholics and those who think they may have a problem with alcohol.

Open-Mindedness: Open-mindedness is the "O" in H.O.W. it works. Without open-mindedness, we cannot make the changes in our thinking and perceptions that are necessary to achieve sobriety. See also "H.O.W. It Works."

Oxford Group: A spiritual, nondenominational, evangelical movement founded in 1921 by a Lutheran minister, Dr. Frank Buchman. AA began as part of the Oxford Group. Bill Wilson wrote that "Early A.A. got its ideas of self-examination, acknowledgment of character defects, restitution for harm done, and working with others straight from the Oxford Groups. . . ."[37] Both Bill Wilson and Dr. Bob were members of the Oxford Group at the time of AA's founding.

P

People, Places, and Things: Prior to recovery, we depended upon people, places, and things to make us happy or to change our lives. In recovery, we take that responsibility away from external events and place it on ourselves. The Twelve and Twelve says, "It is a spiritual axiom that every time we are disturbed, no matter what the cause, there is something wrong *with us.*"[38] See also "People, Places, and Things" in chapter 14, "Use AA Slogans," for more information.

Periodic: An alcoholic who stays sober for a period of time, loses control, goes on a spree, and then repeats the cycle. A periodic alcoholic is to be contrasted to a daily drinker or to one who drinks regularly without significant dry periods. The author of Big Book story number two, "He Had to Be Shown," was a periodic (page 197) as was "The European Drinker" (page 233).

Pigeon: A slang word often used to mean sponsee. The term may also refer to someone new in the program. Dr. Bob himself probably coined the word. One AA member recalled that "Doc would often announce at a meeting, 'There's a pigeon in Room so-and-so who needs some attention.'"[39] According to Lois Wilson, Bill's wife, the use of the term "pigeon" came from AA's earliest days and was consistently used with great affection. In Akron and Cleveland, it was customary to refer to new prospects as "babies," also used with a sense of affectionate care.[40]

Pink Cloud: The feelings of happiness, well-being, and joyous confidence that often characterize those who are new to AA and sobriety. The pink cloud usually comes to an end, after which it is time for the hard work of the AA program. Some of us believe that the pink cloud is a preview of coming attractions for those in AA who are willing to put forth the effort to work the Steps.

Pitch: A term used in some parts of the United States to mean a leader's opening remarks in an AA meeting. It usually lasts five to ten minutes and introduces the discussion topic.

Power Greater than Ourselves: See "Higher Power."

Powerlessness: See "Lack of Power."

Prayer and Meditation: AA's Eleventh Step calls for "prayer and meditation" as a way of improving our conscious contact with God as we understand Him. A handy distinction between prayer and meditation is this: prayer is speaking to God, as we understand Him, whereas meditation is listening to Him.

Preamble: See "AA Preamble."

Primary Purpose: See "AA's Primary Purpose."

Principles Before Personalities: Our recovery from alcoholism is based on AA principles, not on AA personalities. It is the principles of the program, not its personalities, that guide recovery and keep us sober. We rely on the Twelve Steps and their principles rather than on one individual or group of individuals. Individuals, being human, may disappoint us or unintentionally lead us astray. Our ultimate reliance is on our Higher Power.

Program, the: The phrase refers to AA's Twelve Step program of recovery and, more generally, to AA itself. In the South, East, Midwest, and Southwest, AA members speak of being "in" the program. In the West, the expression is "on" the program. When someone keeps slipping and returning to AA, they are said to be "around" the program.

Progress Not Perfection: We seek to make progress rather than to achieve perfection in our AA program and in our lives. When we try to do things perfectly, we are trying to do the impossible. Perfectionism is a reflection of alcoholic grandiosity. The phrase is taken from chapter 5 of the Big Book, "We claim spiritual progress rather than spiritual perfection."[41] It also appears in the Twelve and Twelve, "We shall look for progress, not for perfection."[42]

Progressive Disease: See "Alcoholism as a Progressive Disease."

Promises: See "Twelve Promises."

Q

Qualification: The opening comments that a leader makes in an AA meeting. "Qualification" is generally used in the eastern United States to mean a ten to twenty-minute introduction that entails a brief description of what our drinking days were like, what brought us into AA, and what our life is like now. The qualification is an abbreviated version of "telling our story." A discussion topic for the meeting is taken from the qualification.

R

Recovered Alcoholic: See "Recovered Alcoholic versus Recovering Alcoholic."

Recovered Alcoholic versus Recovering Alcoholic: Some members of Alcoholics Anonymous call themselves "recovering" alcoholics whereas other members call themselves "recovered" alcoholics. Those who use the term "recovering" do so because recovery is an ongoing process that is never complete. Those who use "recovered" do so because they see themselves as having recovered from alcoholism for the one day in which they find themselves. AA literature uses the term "recovered." The foreword to the first edition of the Big Book opens with this sentence: "We, of Alcoholics Anonymous, are more than one hundred men and women who have recovered from a seemingly hopeless state of mind and body. To show other alcoholics *precisely how we have recovered* is the main purpose of this book."[43] See "What Is the Difference Between a 'Recovering' and a 'Recovered' Alcoholic?" in chapter 23, "Common Questions about Alcohol and AA," for more information.

Recovering Alcoholic: See "Recovered Alcoholic versus Recovering Alcoholic."

Rehab: A slang word for a treatment center specializing in alcoholism and other drug addiction treatment. The word is shortened from "rehabilitation center."

Relapse: See "Slip."

Resentments: Feelings of ill will that we hold for others. In recovery, we cannot afford to harbor resentments because they corrode our lives and can lead us back to active alcoholism. The Big Book says, "It is plain that a life which includes deep resentment leads only to futility and unhappiness. To the precise extent that we permit these, do we squander the hours that might have been worth while." [44] The Big Book also reminds us of the source of our resentments. "Being convinced that self, manifested in various ways, was what had defeated us, we considered its common manifestations. Resentment is the 'number one' offender. . . . From it stem all forms of spiritual disease, for we have been not only mentally and physically ill, we have been spiritually sick." [45] See also "Justifiable Anger."

Rigorous Honesty: Complete honesty that does not harm anyone else. AA recovery is based on our being rigorously honest with ourselves and others. Rigorous honesty is sometimes less-than-perfect honesty (we don't necessarily tell a friend wearing a new dress that the dress looks awful) but it is more than technical honesty (half-truths technically true but misleading). Recognizing when we are wrong, admitting our mistakes, making amends, owning up to our self-destructive acts, and recognizing our character defects are all painful actions associated with rigorous self-honesty. The expression "rigorous honesty" comes from chapter 5 of the Big Book, "They [those who do not recover] are naturally incapable of grasping and developing a manner of living which demands rigorous honesty." [46]

Road of Happy Destiny: The road of recovery made possible by the Twelve Steps. The phrase is taken from chapter 11 of the Big Book, "We shall be with you in the Fellowship of the Spirit, and you will surely meet some of us as you trudge the Road of Happy Destiny." [47] The road is "trudged" because recovery requires effort and commitment. Some of the fruits of recovery are summarized in the Twelve Promises and include freedom, peace, and serenity. See "AA Promises" in appendix C, "Often Quoted Passages," for a complete list of the Promises.

Rule 62: The rule is this: Don't take yourself too seriously. The story behind Rule 62 is that in 1940, a super-promoter sobered up in AA. He soon developed a grand scheme for his AA group and applied to AA headquarters in New York for a charter to start three different AA businesses. AA headquarters wrote back that each AA group could handle its own affairs but reminded the promoter "that even less grandiose schemes of a like character had failed everywhere before." [48] Nevertheless, the promoter proceeded with his ideas. He then wrote *sixty-one rules* to ensure that these companies did what they were supposed to do.

When the project failed completely, he wrote AA headquarters to tell them they had been right in the first place. With the letter, he sent a card that he had mailed to every AA group in the country. The card was shaped like a golf card with each group's name and location printed on the front along with the title "Rule No. 62." The card unfolded to reveal a single sentence: "Don't take yourself too damned seriously."[49] The story of Rule 62 is recounted in The Twelve and Twelve, pages 148–149, and in *Alcoholics Anonymous Comes of Age*, pages 103-104.

S

Searching and Fearless Moral Inventory: See "Fourth Step Inventory."

Self-Centeredness: The Big Book says, "Selfishness—self-centeredness! That, we think, is the root of our troubles."[50] According to Bill Wilson, recovery means "destruction of self-centeredness."[51] The Twelve Steps help us achieve that goal. See also "Alcoholic Grandiosity" and "Self-Will Run Riot."

Self-Knowledge Is Not the Answer: We cannot achieve sobriety solely on the basis of knowledge about ourselves and the disease of alcoholism. It takes something more: working the Twelve Steps. The Big Book states, "But the actual or potential alcoholic, with hardly an exception, will be *absolutely unable to stop drinking on the basis of self-knowledge. This is a point we wish to empha-*size and re-emphasize. . . ."[52]

Self-Pity: Feeling sorry for ourselves and dwelling on our own problems. Self-pity increases our misery and can lead us back to drinking. The remedy for self-pity is to get out of ourselves by working with others, especially alcoholics new to AA. Or we can make a gratitude list instead of "getting on the pity pot."

Self-Seeking Will Slip Away: This characteristic is one of AA's Twelve Promises that will come true for those who work the AA program. The promise means that we will seek to help others and to follow God's will for our lives rather than to seek fulfillment of our own selfish wants.

Self-Supporting through Our Own Contributions: The expression is taken from AA's preamble, "There are no dues or fees for A.A. membership; we are self-supporting through our own contributions." See also "Seventh Tradition."

Self-Will Run Riot: The phrase is taken from chapter 5 of the Big Book, "Selfishness—self-centeredness! That, we think, is the root of our troubles. . . . So our troubles, we think, are basically of our own making. They arise out of ourselves, and the alcoholic is an extreme example of self-will run riot, though he usually doesn't think so. Above everything, we alcoholics must be rid of this selfishness. We must, or it kills us!"[53] What is the solution? Working the Twelve Steps and a spiritual awakening.

Serenity Prayer: The Serenity Prayer reads, "God, grant me the serenity to accept the things I cannot change, the courage to change the things I can, and the wisdom to know the difference." This prayer is a powerful tool for finding peace and balance when events and emotions threaten to overwhelm us. When we are frightened, angry, impatient, lonely, or tempted to drink, repeating its words has a soothing effect. See chapter 10, "Use the Serenity Prayer," for more information.

Service: Service is one of AA's Three Legacies. The Big Book states, "Our real purpose is to fit ourselves to be of maximum service to God and the people about us."[54] Bill Wilson said, "A.A. is more than a set of principles; it is a society of recovered alcoholics in action. We *must* carry A.A.'s message; otherwise we ourselves may fall into decay and those who have not yet been given the truth may die. This is why we so often say that *action* is the magic word. Action to carry A.A.'s message is therefore the heart of our Third Legacy of Service."[55]

Seventh Tradition: "Every A.A. group ought to be fully self-supporting, declining outside contributions." As a result of this Tradition, Alcoholics Anonymous accepts contributions *only* from its members. However, there are no dues or fees for AA membership. (AA headquarters restricts annual gifts and bequests from an AA member to a maximum of one thousand dollars. Anything over that amount from an AA member or any amount at all from a non-AA member is politely refused.)

Sharing: The process by which AA members share with each other their experience, strength, and hope concerning alcoholism and recovery. The great discovery of Bill Wilson and Dr. Bob was that such sharing could help an alcoholic stay sober. It is one of the foundations of AA recovery. The term appears in the AA preamble, "Alcoholics Anonymous is a fellowship of men and women who share their experience, strength and hope with each other that they may solve their common problem and help others to recover from alcoholism."

Shotgun Sobriety: As the phrase suggests, this type of sobriety is based on fear of drinking rather than on the application of AA principles. All of us in recovery have a healthy respect for the power of alcohol, but we do not have to live in terror of it. Long-term sobriety is based on spiritual principles, not on fear of booze.

Simple Program: AA, it has been said, is a simple program for complicated people. AA's Twelve Step program is simple because it works simply: one Step at a time, one day at a time. Because it is simple, however, does not mean that it is easy. Working the program requires dedication and effort. Yet the strength and courage to work the Steps are given to all those who ask for them. The phrase "simple program" is taken from chapter 5 of the Big Book, "Those who do not recover are people who cannot or will not completely give themselves to this simple program, usually men and women who are constitutionally incapable of being honest with themselves."[56] See also "Constitutionally Incapable of Being Honest." Refer to "Keep It Simple" in chapter 14, "Use AA slogans," for more information.

Slip: To drink alcohol again after a period of sobriety in AA. The word can also be used as a noun. The technical term for a slip is "relapse." Relapse is often part of recovery, but it does not have to be. S.L.I.P. is sometimes used as an acronym: Sobriety Loses Its Priority.

Slippery Places: To slip is to drink again after a period of sobriety in AA. "Slippery places" refer to actual places or to emotional states and situations in which we are more likely to drink again. A slippery place is anywhere a special temptation to drink exists because of old habits, friends, memories, pressures, emotions, or just the availability of alcohol. Unless we have a legitimate reason to be there, we avoid slippery places. See chapter 13, "Avoid Slippery Places," for more information.

Smith, Anne Ripley: The wife of AA cofounder Dr. Robert Smith. It was she who got Dr. Bob to attend the Oxford Group meetings[57] and who nourished AA with her love and care from its earliest days. A graduate of Wellesley College, she played a major role in the founding of AA.

Smith, Robert Holbrook, M.D. ("Dr. Bob"): Cofounder with Bill Wilson of Alcoholics Anonymous. Dr. Bob was born on August 8, 1879, in St. Johnsbury, Vermont and died on November 16, 1950. He graduated from Dartmouth College and from the Rush Medical School in Chicago after significant misadventures with alcohol. Dr. Bob was a well-respected and capable proctologist and rectal surgeon (when sober) whose temperament and outlook were complementary to those of Bill Wilson, his cofounder and sponsor.[58]

Dr. Bob created the first AA group in the world, Akron Group Number One, in Akron, Ohio. (Bill Wilson created AA Group Number Two in New York City.) Dr. Bob was sober from June 10, 1935, the official date of the founding of AA, until his death. He is referred to as "Doc" in the Big Book. His biography, *Dr. Bob and the Good Oldtimers: A Biography, with Recollections of Early A.A. in the Midwest,* has been published by AA. See appendix A, "A Brief History of Alcoholics Anonymous," for more information.

Sobriety Date: The date on which we had our last drink. It is the date we got sober.

Speaker's Meeting: An AA meeting that features one or two speakers who share their experience, strength, and hope for the entire meeting. The speakers talk about what it was like while they were drinking, what brought them into AA, and what their lives are like now.

Spiritual Awakening: See "Spiritual Awakening/Spiritual Experience."

Spiritual Awakening/Spiritual Experience: Some AA members have a spiritual experience whereas others undergo a spiritual awakening as the result of working the Twelve Steps. The Big Book describes both a spiritual awakening and a spiritual experience as a "personality change sufficient to bring about recovery from alcoholism."[59] It also describes them as a "profound alteration in [our] reaction to life"[60] and as an "awareness of a Power greater than ourselves."[61] The difference between an awakening and an experience is simply timing: how long it takes. See chapter 6, "Say Your Prayers," for a more detailed discussion.

Spiritual Experience: See "Spiritual Awakening/Spiritual Experience."

Spiritual Tool Kit: The phrase refers to the spiritual tools that the AA program makes available to help us stay sober. These tools include the Twelve Steps, reliance on a Power greater than ourselves, and prayer and meditation. The term comes from chapter 2 of the Big Book: "There was nothing left for us but to pick up the simple kit of spiritual tools laid at our feet."[62] It also appears in chapter 7 of the Big Book: "Simply lay out the kit of spiritual tools for his [the alcoholic's] inspection. Show him how they worked with you."[63]

Sponsor: An AA member who serves as a personal tutor, guide, confidante, and friend to another person in the AA program. A sponsor helps a sponsee work the Twelve Steps; shares his or her personal experience, strength, and hope; and helps the sponsee stay on the recovery track. A sponsor is a crucial part of recovery. See chapter 5, "Call Your Sponsor," for a more detailed discussion of sponsorship.

Step Study Meeting: An AA meeting that focuses on a study of the Twelve Steps, usually at the rate of one Step per meeting.

Steps: See "Twelve Steps."

Stinking Thinking: The phrase refers to old thought patterns and perceptions which, when they occur in recovery, can lead us back to drinking. Some examples of "stinking thinking" are blaming others, fault-finding, alcoholic grandiosity, skipping meetings, self-centeredness, and taking other people's inventory while refusing to look at our own defects. "Stinking thinking" is a warning sign that we are not working our AA program.

Surrender: To surrender in AA is to take the first Three Steps. It means: (1) admitting that we are powerless over alcohol and that our lives have become unmanageable, (2) coming to believe that a Power greater than ourselves could restore us to sanity, and (3) turning our will and our lives over to the care of God as we understand Him. Surrender is the key to recovery. By hitting bottom and giving up, we find our alcoholic egos deflated. Then we are open to a Power greater than ourselves to restore us to sanity. Until we accept our powerlessness over alcohol and become willing to do the Steps, we cannot find recovery in AA. Bill Wilson wrote, "Such is the paradox of A.A. regeneration: strength arising out of complete defeat and weakness, the loss of one's old life as a condition for finding a new one."[64] See also "Lack of Power."

T

Terminally Unique: An alcoholic's idea that he or she is so "unique" as to require special treatment in AA that exempts him or her from some part of the AA program or the Twelve Steps. See also "Alcoholic Grandiosity."

Thirteenth Step: There is no thirteenth step in AA. The term is used to describe inappropriate sexual advances made by one member of the Fellowship toward newcomers or other AA members (such as sponsors toward sponsees). It is used in a negative sense.

Thirteenth Stepping: See "Thirteenth Step."

Three Legacies of AA: The Three Legacies of Alcoholics Anonymous are Recovery, Unity, and Service. These legacies are so-called because they have been passed down to us from the cofounders and old-timers of AA. The Legacy of Recovery is contained in the Big Book, the Twelve Steps, and Twelfth Step work. The Legacy of Unity is contained in the Twelve Traditions. Of this Legacy, Bill Wilson said, "We can do together what I cannot do alone."[65] The Legacy of Service is contained in every act which helps AA function or which carries the AA message to those who need it.[66]

Traditions: See "Twelve Traditions."

Treatment Center: A center specializing in the treatment of alcoholism and other drug addictions.

Twelfth Step Call: To make a Twelfth Step call is to carry the AA message of recovery to an alcoholic *who is still drinking*. See chapter 7, "Help Another Alcoholic," for more information.

Twelfth Step Work: The term refers to carrying the AA message of recovery to another alcoholic. Twelfth Step work includes making Twelfth Step calls (carrying the AA message of recovery to an alcoholic *who is still drinking*). But it includes more. We do Twelfth Step work whenever we carry the message to an alcoholic, even when that alcoholic is in recovery. For example, by attending AA meetings; sharing our experience, strength, and hope with others in meetings and outside meetings; sponsoring; and performing service work of all kinds. The term comes from AA's Twelfth Step which asks us to carry the message of AA recovery to other alcoholics.

Twelve and Twelve: See *"Twelve Steps and Twelve Traditions."*

"Twelve Concepts for World Service": The Twelve Concepts form the basis of AA's structure and describe how the various parts of Alcoholics Anonymous

(AA groups, General Service Conference, General Service Board, General Service Office, and so on) work together.[67] These practical service principles for Alcoholics Anonymous, including the spiritual principles which form their basis, were published in booklet form in 1962.[68]

Twelve Promises: A list of benefits that AA members receive from having painstakingly worked the first nine Steps of the AA program. Included among the Promises are a "new freedom," a "new happiness," "serenity," and "peace." See "AA Promises" in appendix C, "Often Quoted Passages," for the complete list of Promises.

Twelve Step Call: See "Twelfth Step Call."

Twelve Step Work: See "Twelfth Step Work."

Twelve Stepping: The term refers to making a Twelfth Step call or doing Twelfth Step work. It also means to work all Twelve Steps rather than just the First Step and part of the Twelfth Step while skipping those in between. See also "Two Stepper" and "Twelfth Step Calls."

Twelve Steps: "A.A.'s Twelve Steps are a group of principles, spiritual in their nature, which, if practiced as a way of life, can expel the obsession to drink and enable the sufferer to become happily and usefully whole."[69] The Steps were written by Bill Wilson on the basis of the experience of the first one hundred members of AA and were approved by the AA groups after slight modification. The Twelve Steps are the basis of the AA program of recovery. See chapter 4, "Work the Steps," for more information.

Twelve Steps and Twelve Traditions: The title of a collection of essays in book form published in 1952 by Alcoholics Anonymous. It is an important supplement to the Big Book because of its detailed treatment of the Twelve Steps and its discussion of the Twelve Traditions. The book was written by Bill Wilson. It is affectionately called the Twelve and Twelve.

Twelve Traditions: "A.A.'s Twelve Traditions apply to the life of the Fellowship itself. They outline the means by which A.A. maintains its unity and relates itself to the world about it, the way it lives and grows."[70] The Twelve Traditions of AA give the Fellowship its form, substance, and unity.[71] They "are to group survival and harmony what A.A.'s Twelve Steps are to each member's sobriety and peace of mind."[72]

Two Stepper: Slang for an AA member who works only the First Step and part of the Twelfth Step, but none of the Steps in between. Two-stepping looks like an "easier, softer way," but it is not. To shortcut AA's Twelve Step program by two-stepping eliminates the heart of the work of recovery. The resulting sobriety is therefore shaky.

Two-Stepping: See "Two Stepper."

U

Unity: AA's Second Legacy of Service. See "Three Legacies of AA."

Unmanageability: In the first Step, we admit not only that we are powerless over alcohol, but that our lives have become unmanageable. Only by recognizing the unmanageability of our lives can we open ourselves to changing the way we live them. Refer to chapter 4, "Work the Steps," for more information.

W

Wet Brain: An alcoholic whose drinking has caused such permanent brain damage that he or she can no longer function in society and has to be institutionalized for the remainder of his or her life.

White Knuckle Sobriety: A desperate effort to stay sober through the exercise of willpower rather than through an act of surrender and the Twelve Steps.

Willingness: The "W" in H.O.W. It Works. Unless we are willing to listen, to change, and to work the Steps, we won't be able to stay sober in AA. Many of us have found that we had to pray for willingness in order to become willing.

Wilson, Bill: Cofounder with Dr. Robert Smith of Alcoholics Anonymous. William Griffith Wilson was born November 26, 1895, in East Dorset Vermont, in a room behind a bar[73] and died on January 24, 1971.

Bill never graduated from college, but he earned a law degree studying nights at the Brooklyn Law School, graduating in 1924. "After paying the fifteen-dollar fee for his diploma, he was too drunk to leave the apartment the next day to pick it up. He never bothered to get it."[74] Bill's last drink was on December 11, 1934.

Bill is the author of AA's Twelve Steps, the Twelve Traditions, the Big Book (except for the stories), *The Twelve Steps and Twelve Traditions, Alcoholics Anonymous Comes of Age,* and *As Bill Sees It.* His biography, *'Pass It On,'* has been published by AA. See appendix A, "A Brief History of Alcoholics Anonymous," for more information about Bill Wilson and AA's founding.

GLOSSARY ENDNOTES

1. *Inside A.A.: Understanding the Fellowship and Its Service Agencies* (New York: AA World Services, Inc., 1974), *The Twelve Concepts for World Service Illustrated* (New York: Alcoholics Anonymous World Services, Inc., 1986).

2. Robertson, Nan, *Getting Better: Inside Alcoholics Anonymous* (New York: Fawcett Crest Book published by Ballantine Books, 1988), 88.

3. *Alcoholics Anonymous,* 3d ed. (New York: Alcoholics Anonymous World Services, Inc., 1976), 60.

4. *This Is A.A.: An Introduction to the A.A. Recovery Program* (New York: Alcoholics Anonymous World Services, Inc., 1984), 9.

5. *Alcoholics Anonymous,* 64.

6. *Alcoholics Anonymous,* 58.

7. *Alcoholics Anonymous,* 76.

8. *Alcoholics Anonymous,* 63.

9. *Twelve Steps and Twelve Traditions* (New York: Alcoholics Anonymous World Services, Inc., 1952), 34–35.

10. *Alcoholics Anonymous,* 58.

11. *Twelve Steps and Twelve Traditions,* 96.

12. *Alcoholics Anonymous,* 58.

13. *Alcoholics Anonymous,* 570.

14. *Alcoholics Anonymous,* 30.

15. *Alcoholics Anonymous,* 30.

16. *Alcoholics Anonymous,* 58–59.

17. *Alcoholics Anonymous,* 85.

18. *Alcoholics Anonymous,* 28.

19. *Alcoholics Anonymous,* 19.

20. *Alcoholics Anonymous,* 76.

21. *Alcoholics Anonymous,* 94.

22. *Alcoholics Anonymous,* 59.

23. *Alcoholics Anonymous,* 133.

24. *Twelve Steps and Twelve Traditions,* 24.

25. Kurtz, Ernest, *Not-God: A History of Alcoholics Anonymous,* rev. ed. (Center City, Minn.: Hazelden Educational Materials, 1991), 61.

26. *Alcoholics Anonymous,* 570.

27. *Twelve Steps and Twelve Traditions,* 153.

28. *Twelve Steps and Twelve Traditions,* 72.

29. *As Bill Sees It: The A.A. Way of Life . . . Selected Writings of A.A.'s Co-Founder* (New York: Alcoholics Anonymous World Services, Inc., 1980), 106.

30. *Twelve Steps and Twelve Traditions,* 70.

31. *As Bill Sees It,* 332.

32. Kurtz, Ernest, *Not-God,* 61.

33. *Alcoholics Anonymous Comes of Age: A Brief History of A.A.* (New York: Alcoholics Anonymous World Services, Inc., 1957), 139.

34. *Twelve Steps and Twelve Traditions,* 90.

35. *Alcoholics Anonymous,* 45.

36. *Alcoholics Anonymous,* 77.

37. *Alcoholics Anonymous Comes of Age,* 39.

38. *Twelve Steps and Twelve Traditions,* 90.

39. *Dr. Bob and the Good Oldtimers: A Biography, with Recollections of Early A.A. in the Midwest* (New York: Alcoholics Anonymous World Services, Inc., 1980), 146.
40. Kurtz, Ernest, *Not-God*, 39.
41. *Alcoholics Anonymous*, 60.
42. *Twelve Steps and Twelve Traditions*, 91.
43. *Alcoholics Anonymous*, xiii.
44. *Alcoholics Anonymous*, 66.
45. *Alcoholics Anonymous*, 64.
46. *Alcoholics Anonymous*, 58.
47. *Alcoholics Anonymous*, 164.
48. Kurtz, Ernest, *Not-God*, 107.
49. *Alcoholics Anonymous Comes of Age*, 103–4.
50. *Alcoholics Anonymous*, 62.
51. *Alcoholics Anonymous*, 14.
52. *Alcoholics Anonymous*, 39.
53. *Alcoholics Anonymous*, 62.
54. *Alcoholics Anonymous*, 77.
55. *Alcoholics Anonymous Comes of Age*, 139–40.
56. *Alcoholics Anonymous*, 58.
57. *Dr. Bob and the Good Oldtimers*, 55.
58. *Dr. Bob and the Good Oldtimers*, 33, 125.
59. *Alcoholics Anonymous*, 569.
60. *Alcoholics Anonymous*, 569.
61. *Alcoholics Anonymous*, 570.
62. *Alcoholics Anonymous*, 25.
63. *Alcoholics Anonymous*, 95.
64. *As Bill Sees It*, 49.
65. *'Pass It On,' The Story of Bill Wilson and How the A.A. Message Reached the World* (New York: Alcoholics Anonymous World Services, Inc., 1984), 347.
66. *Alcoholics Anonymous Comes of Age*, 139–40.
67. *The Twelve Concepts for World Service Illustrated* (New York: Alcoholics Anonymous World Services, Inc., 1986).
68. *Lois Remembers* (New York: Al-Anon Family Group Headquarters, Inc., 1979), 158.
69. *Twelve Steps and Twelve Traditions*, 15.
70. *Twelve Steps and Twelve Traditions*, 15.
71. *Twelve Steps and Twelve Traditions*, 18.
72. *Alcoholics Anonymous Comes of Age*, 96.
73. *'Pass It On,'* 13.
74. *Lois Remembers*, 31.

General Index

Index to Slogans

A

Accept life on life's terms, 48–49

Avoid slippery places, 3, 46–47, 121

C

Call your sponsor, 3, 22–26

Carry the message, 34

D

Do the next right thing, 121

Don't drink, 3, 5–6, 121

E

Easing God Out (E.G.O.), 53

Easy does it . . . but do it, 49

F

First things first, 121

G

Go to meetings, 3, 7–10

Go with the flow, 54

H

H.A.L.T., 46, 121

Help another alcoholic, 3, 32–34

How It Works—H: Honesty,
O: Open-mindedness,
W: Willingness, 4

I

I can't, God can, I think I'll let Him, 16

It works if you work it, 48

J

Just for today, 108

K

K.I.S.S. *See* Keep it simple

Keep coming back, 48, 49

Keep it simple, 3, 50, 121

L

Let go and let God, 50–51, 121

Live and let live, 51, 121

N

Ninety in ninety, 7

O

One day at a time, 3, 37–38, 107, 121

One drink is too many and a thousand drinks are not enough, 6

Other titles that will interest you. . .

Twenty-Four Hours a Day

Millions of people worldwide open this little book each morning to guide their recovery—one day at a time. For over forty years this classic has been offering daily thoughts, meditations, and prayers for living well and staying sober. 400 pp.
Order No. 5093

The Little Red Book

One of the most-used and best-loved study companions to the Big Book, *Alcoholics Anonymous,* this little book offers those of us new to recovery—or seeking a deeper meaning in the Twelve Steps—advice on program work, sponsorship, spirituality, and much more. This wealth of knowledge offers support, encouragement, and wisdom in the search for serenity and sobriety. 154 pp.
Order No. 1034

A Program for You

A Guide to the Big Book's Design for Living

Written in today's language, this study guide interprets the original AA program as described in *Alcoholics Anonymous.* It serves as the basic study guide to the Big Book and helps us apply the Twelve Steps to our lives. 183 pp.
Order No. 5122

For price and order information, or a free catalog, please call our Telephone Representatives.

HAZELDEN

1-800-328-0098	**1-612-257-4010**	**1-612-257-1331**
(Toll Free. U.S., Canada, and the Virgin Islands)	(Outside the U.S. and Canada)	(24-Hour FAX)

Pleasant Valley Road • P.O. Box 176 • Center City, MN 55012-0176